Sacred Outrage

Sacred Outrage

A Seasoned Woman's Guide to Soulful Citizen Action

Mary Knapp

Foreword by Andrew Harvey

Wisdom Moon Publishing
2015

SACRED OUTRAGE

A SEASONED WOMAN'S GUIDE TO SOULFUL CITIZEN ACTION

Published by Wisdom Moon Publishing LLC

Wisdom Moon™ , the Wisdom Moon logo™ , *Wisdom Moon Publishing* ™ , and *WMP* ™ are trademarks of Wisdom Moon Publishing LLC.

www.WisdomMoonPublishing.com

ISBN 978-1-938459-58-0 (softcover, alk. paper)
ISBN 978-1-938459-61-0 (eBook)

LCCN 2015951938

Front-cover design a joint project of Wisdom Moon Publishing, LLC, and Rolf Fredenberg.

TABLE OF CONTENTS

Dedication

This book is dedicated to a woman I've never met. I don't even know her name.

A few years ago my husband and I ran away to Prague for a long weekend. We roamed about the quaint city soaking up its food, its friendly folks, and its lively cultural atmosphere.

On our last day we visited the Museum of Communism. Situated between a McDonald's on one side and a casino on the other, the museum houses a painful glimpse into what life had been like for people who lived behind the Iron Curtain. I spent hours taking in the artifacts, paintings, videos, documents, music, and old photographs.

There was one photograph that seized me profoundly, body, mind, and spirit, and I stood for the longest time, absorbing it.

It had been taken in 1968 during "The Prague Spring" when people began to express their unhappiness and discontent, their agitation and unrest. Calls began for government reform, more freedom, and independence.

The Soviet Union, and its coalition, responded by ultimately sending in half a million troops and tanks to occupy the streets, to insinuate themselves in, around, and among the people.

Citizens fell out into the streets to object to the sudden occupation. Heavy tanks rolled through cobbled streets topped high, and spilling over, with heavily-armed soldiers. Giant fire hoses power-washed people clean off the streets and sidewalks. Shots were fired. People scattered. Smoke rose. People lay dead.

In the one particular photo that so struck me, there was a wall of soldiers wearing gas masks, standing shoulder-to-shoulder, the width of the street and a block deep. They were lined up sharply, precisely spaced, at strict attention, tense hands gripping their sub-machine guns.

In front of them, within arm's length, stood a woman, an older woman, dressed smartly in a buttoned-up tweed overcoat, hand gloves, and sensible shoes.

She stood before this massive wall of intimidating military might, hands clasped in front of her, pocketbook dangling from her forearm. Staring them down. Calmly. Relaxed. Unflinchingly focused. Undeterred, she had taken it upon herself to take action, and stood there resolutely between the soldiers and her beloved people.

It is to this seasoned woman that I dedicate this book.

I also dedicate it to all Seasoned Women everywhere who share this same spirit, who are boldly summoning their courage, calling up their power and almighty might, who are focused, undeterred, and unflinching in taking determined action to stand resolutely against the harm that is being inflicted on all our beloved people and upon this beautiful planet.

Foreword by Andrew Harvey

Mary Knapp is a woman of great passion and courage; she is not afraid to take a stand and to speak out. At this time, when the world is facing so many catastrophic crises, Mary is the kind of leader we need to listen to.

She has spent her life caring deeply about the well being of others and building communities where everyone can have an opportunity to grow and develop to their fullest potential.

In our contemporary world, where there are so many dangers present and so much free-floating anger on the loose, Mary shows us how to use the energy of anger in a way that it is positive, constructive, and that brings about the kinds of changes needed.

She specifically calls upon women elders to take action in their local communities to lead others in transmuting anger into intentional right action. Women elders are the ideal ones to show us the way forward and out of this mess we've gotten ourselves into. They possess the precise kinds of skills, experience, knowledge, wisdom, and clear vision needed for these times. Women elders have spent their lives building communities, nurturing life, fostering love, and extending their embrace of compassion to include all sentient beings.

This book is a step-by-step guide into the kind of action women elders can take to bring together our communities to create solutions to our challenges.

Foreword

The first part of this book lays out in brutal honesty the dire state of our current social, political, economic, and environmental crises, along with the conditions that brought us to this historical crossroad.

Mary discusses the important issues that need addressing and outlines exactly what is needed to address them.

Then, using a holistic approach, Mary presents a how-to manual for women elders to go into their communities and bring together all the different interconnecting parts of society: government, nongovernmental organizations, business, faith communities, educators, the media, the arts, and private citizens, to work towards addressing our most urgent challenges.

What you have here is a practical guide for women elders to step up and step forward, firmly, and with great love, to begin where we live, within our local communities, using precise, time-proven community-building methods.

Mary balances a deep love for others with a fierce compassion-in-action towards firmly relieving the rampant cruelty, suffering and destruction brought on by carelessness, greed and ignorance. She provides women elders with the inspiration, the hope and the exact tools needed to go into their communities to create social, political, economic and environmental solutions that are good for everyone.

For all those who are waking up and daring to dream another world into being, Mary has given the world a superb handbook to assist us. In answering our calls to become powerful leaders and to influence our communities positively, her book gives us the know-how and the confidence to do so wisely, well, and for the betterment of everyone.

Andrew Harvey,
author of *The Hope: A Guide to Sacred Activism.*

Introduction

I was not prepared for how deeply I would fall in love when having my children. Their innocence and vulnerability ignited in me a fierce sense of protectiveness and an unwavering sense of responsibility. Motherhood evoked a sense of wonder and awe over the mystery of life and creation and I have never been able to look again, in quite the same way, at the earth, the stars, ants, oceans, and the sparkles of light dancing atop waves under a blaze of sun. Everywhere I see the interconnecting web of life, humans, plants, animals, ecosystems, all existing in balance to everything and everyone else.

My children are grown now and having children of their own, but still I look out upon the world with the same awe, the same reverence for creation, and with the same fierce sense of protectiveness.

I also look out upon the world and see that we are living in a time when the worst thing that has ever happened on earth is happening now, politically, socially, economically, environmentally, and it is we humans who have caused it. I see that we are at a crossroads between survival and extinction. And that we have allowed the world to become a hostile and uninhabitable place for all our children and everyone's grandchildren.

I look out upon this beautiful, but beleaguered world and for the sake of all sentient beings, feel called to do something. Compelled. Summoned. I recognize a moral mandate here.

**There are things that need protecting.
There are things that need defending so that they can survive.**

There are a great many of us Seasoned Women who are now experiencing a convergence of different aspects of our lives. With childrearing behind us, we are free to pursue other creative interests. Our lifelong nurturing has become directed outward and is infinitely more inclusive of so many and so much more. Through home and work, we have lived long lives of cooperating within systems of interrelating parts. Through our feminine energy, we easily experience ourselves as vessels of spirit. We are clear in our vision and have a heightened sense of social inequities. We have the time, the energy, the resources, skills, ability, wisdom, and desire to take action to create a safe, healthy and sustainable world.

Just as we Seasoned Women have developed great capacities for gentle love and tender compassion, so, too, have we developed a heightened inability to tolerate cruelty, violence, harm; injustice, inequality, and unfairness.

Anger is a most appropriate response to the untold destruction, cruelty, pain, and suffering being imposed upon the tender beings of this fragile earth by those who are careless, ignorant, greedy, or just plain evil.

What is *NOT* an appropriate response would be the kind of anger that is loosed wildly, violently, out of control; the kind of anger that burns down entire forests, destroying every green and living creature within a world-wide radius.

There comes a time when righteous anger must be called upon, as fuel, as impetus, as the kick-in-the-butt that's needed to kick-start and drive the kinds of changes that are needed.

We Seasoned Women are feeling the call to haul out our trusty blackened cast iron cauldrons into our open dirt yards, fire them up until they're hot with blue blazes and set to stirring up our special alchemical mix of all the right amounts of ferocity, gentleness, integrity, compassion, strength, nonviolence, powerful deep love and care with a most healthy and generous infusion of

> "Awwwww, hell no!"
> "Enough is enough!"
> "That's it! I've had it up to here!"

A most desirable and much-needed Sacred Outrage is a Seasoned Woman's ability to transmute anger into clear, focused, balanced, powerfully-controlled, intentional right actions for the purpose of bringing forth into this hobbled world the positive, healthy, life-sustaining change that is needed.

For good or ill, like it or not, everyone around the globe is now interconnected socially, politically, technologically, economically, and environmentally. Our challenge is to become Soulful Citizen Activists; to create new ways of living together, communicating, cooperating, sharing information and managing resources.

Seasoned Women were made for just these kinds of times to guide and influence our way forward, to reorient humans to our true and natural position in the world order, to mobilize everyone, of all ages, to become Soulful Citizen Activists, to do their part to bring this world-wide madness to a screeching halt.

Introduction

Seasoned women have developed the very qualities now needed to live in our interdependent world. They are passionately alive in their communities having spent lifetimes building relationships, networking, collaborating, communicating, and getting things done. They are solution-oriented, highly imaginative, long-term visionaries, weaving together the well-being of mates, children, families, workplaces, communities and the environment, keenly attuned to the mystery of life, ever evolving and dynamic.

At this crossroads between survival and extinction, what this sore old world needs most are Seasoned Women answering a deep inner call to action out of a fierce sense of protectiveness, out of a reverence for life and its interconnected web; out of profound love for humanity's children; to bring forth a better life; to cause a swift and gentle correction to our current and unsafe path; to nurture, tend, and care for our deep connections with each other and with the earth.

What this world needs is the clear, focused, balanced, powerfully controlled, intentional right actions of Sacred Outrage.

There are things that need protecting.
There are things that need defending so that they can survive.

CHAPTER ONE

A Matter of Life—Death—Life

Let's get right to it:

There is a huge shift happening! A demographic shift!

The older population is rising higher and faster than any other age group and there are now more older people than younger people.[1]

Of this older population, it is women who make up the majority.

For the first time ever in human history, the sheer number of seasoned women is significant and unprecedented.[2]

In the U.S. there are 40 million of us.

40 MILLION!

We are living longer; are healthy and educated; racially, ethnically, and culturally diverse; active socially and politically; technologically savvy; and we have our own money.

Seasoned Women are now a vast multitude, a living, breathing bona fide "preponderance" which, according to the Merriam-Webster dictionary, means we have now achieved "the quality or fact of being greater in number, quantity, or importance."

What this means is that Seasoned Women are uniquely positioned to bring to bear enormous powers of influence—not just within our families, but in local, national, and international affairs.

1

Fact:

The world is linked together economically, politically, technologically, environmentally, and socially in interconnecting systems, networks, and integrated markets. We cannot escape this.

Fact:

We are living in a time when the worst thing that has ever happened on earth is happening now. The Economic crisis. Depletion of our natural resources. Global warming. An imbalanced ecosystem. Pollution of the air, land, and water. Extinction of animals and sea life. Disease. Hunger. Poverty. Overcrowding. Wars and conflicts over oil, land, water, religion, culture, identity.

Fact:

Solving our urgent global problems requires innovation and ingenuity. The old model of imbalance, competition, exclusion, domination and control no longer serves us. Our challenge is to create new ways of living together, communicating, cooperating, sharing information, and managing resources.

The path forward is understanding that the good life, our greatest joy and deepest need, is based on setting free our innate compassionate natures and consciously contributing to each other's well-being.

Our global community is in a state of great transition. It is an exciting transformation that is trying to take hold for the purposes of advancing us all into progressively higher, deeper, wider, and more richly dimensional ways of relating to each other and to the natural world.

All across the planet, people are feeling this pull to leave behind our current deteriorating mode of existence and create a new and improved one. Like it or not, we are moving through this passage and we are moving through it together whether it be by holding hands and linking up, or by feeling that we are shackled in cold steel chains. Either way, we are in this together. Inescapably. Our freedom comes in choosing which attitudes and what actions we will employ to cross over and bridge this divide.

Some are consciously surrendering to this process of passing from one life into another with an earnest desire to help bring about changes that benefit the good of everyone. Others are unconsciously stuck in temper tantrums, flailing and thrashing about, bellowing and shrieking at the top of their lungs, protesting and digging in their heels. Nonetheless, they, too will make the crossing right along with the rest of us, toes scraping the pavement as they are dragged kicking and screaming, red-faced and furious that global circumstances have escaped their continued control.

At the same time that this is an exciting and exhilarating time to be alive for this great transformation, it is also fraught with great fear. We are seeing what happens when unacknowledged and unmanaged fear is loosed wildly in the world resulting in widespread outbreaks of violence, grave danger, unspeakable acts of cruelty, and brutal attempts to usurp and stop this unstoppable process.

Our old outdated societal institutions and outmoded ways of thinking are being shaken down to their very foundations, until shuddering and lurching hard, they will eventually collapse all around us in heaps and piles. There is much to do to usher in and ease the way for the renovations ahead. Even though we are being summoned into a bright and healthy future, there are many people who are now suffering, confused, bewildered, terrified, and in need of gentle compassion combined with firm, direct action.

The Best Women for the Job

It is Seasoned Women who are the best ones to step forward now into positions of leadership and influence in every important societal and civic area: in politics, nongovernmental organizations, business, education, religion, media, in financial, social, judicial, artistic, psychological, and spiritual domains, and in community. An untapped resource, we are rich in acquired skills, abilities, knowledge, and experience, steeped in hard-won wisdom and God-given talents.

Seasoned Women have spent a lifetime networking, building relationships, collaborating, cooperating, communicating, and cleaning up messes. We know how to get things done. We know how to weave together the well-being of mates, children, family, workplaces, friends, communities, and the environment.

Our backgrounds are chock-full of skills, proficiencies and expertise as working women, mates, mothers, and community members; it reads exactly like the kind of professional resume that qualifies us unequivocally for leadership positions in these challenging times:

- Team building
- Diplomacy
- Flexibility
- Sacrifice
- Resource Management
- Time Management
- Tough decision-making
- Anticipating needs

- Discretion
- Hard work
- Long hours
- Multitasking

Communicating, cooperating, collaborating, we know how to take on difficult issues, generate different ideas and perspectives, broaden the discussion, ask tough questions, and drive on towards direct and detailed answers and solutions.

We are what's needed to step into roles as wise leaders, to rethink our inadequate and failed models of living, and to focus on results with equal attention given to the health and well-being of all people, communities, nations and the earth.

In Grace and Gratitude

Seasoned Women have lived through countless years, days, and moments of laughing, crying, suffering, failing, falling, getting up, and trudging on. We have stared steadily into the cavernous eyes of various abject terrors; breathed and dry-heaved our way through any number of physical and psychic wounds, deep sorrows, crushing defeats, and heavy disappointments. We have mothered others. We have mothered ourselves. We have comforted the sick and the dying, held up and held close those who were broken in body, heart and spirit.

We have loved our way through mates, partners, children, parents, friends, and a vast menagerie of beloved family pets.

We have launched children into the world and ourselves into careers. We have held tight to the reins during rough and rocky rides through financial hardships, pinched a penny till it screamed, made a gallon of milk and Sunday's roast last clear through Wednesday.

Yet still we rose from long nights of restless sleep, dressed in cotton and lace, lit our morning candles in grace and gratitude for another precious day to love, to serve, to feed, and to tend the needs of others—physically, psychologically, socially, and spiritually.

From Out of the Ashes

We women are the keepers of cycles, the endless transmitters and midwives of birth and death and rebirth. We know intimately that to everything there is a season. Our bodies move us constantly through ages and stages, patterns of physical, emotional, and spiritual endings and beginnings, ebbs and flows, rises and falls, releasing and letting go that which does not serve us, letting die what needs to die, and then opening up always to be renewed and revivified.

We find ourselves in a world in the midst of a death stage on this life-death-life continuum. A world sputtering, gasping, in need of letting our current maladaptive lifestyle and belief system burn out so that a new world can rise up out of the ashes, one that will nourish the many, and not just a few.

There's a new world trying to be born, to come forth and take form, trying to emerge from out of the old and broken world that is decaying and passing away. It is Seasoned Women who are especially equipped to step forward and gently, tenderly, lovingly—firmly—midwife it into being.

What Seasoned Women Want

Women elders and their unique way of knowing have been alive forever in the deep collective unconscious of the human psyche, simultaneously in touch with this world and the other worlds.

At our age, we are still diving eagerly and often, ever-deeper into the pool of consciousness, splashing about merrily in this body of holy waters where the Physical swirls with the Divine. Where Spirit and Matter meet. We are there. Immersed. In a synchronized swim, bobbing, gliding, floating, gamboling; doing cannon balls, torpedoes, and watermelons.

When it comes to navigating the waters where Spirit and Matter mix, Seasoned Women are Master Divers, keen to recover with great zeal something that has been lost to all of us for far too long—a sense of the sacred.

The pockets of Seasoned Women are bulging with boundless wisdom, stores of knowledge, and priceless information. We possess a keen awareness and refined senses of what is happening and what needs to happen. We see what we see and know what we know.

Like warm, healing honey, Seasoned Women long to pour their hard-won wisdom over the wounds of the world.

As Seasoned Women, we want our lives to have mattered. We long to infuse the world with our unique and special contribution, pulling it back from the edge of a most steep and jagged cliff. We yearn to make a difference, to participate in nursing the planet back to life; to reorient humans to their true and natural place on the earth and in the scheme of the universe.

Seasoned Women are bursting to be of service, to spend our hearts and energies lavishly, easing the passing of an old dying world and nurturing the birth and growth of the new one.

Even after a lifetime of loving others, Seasoned Women go on fathoming new depths of what it means to love. Like a breeze that sweeps across a still lake, the love we feel has rippled out past just children, mates, and community, farther and farther, until now it has come to include all of humanity and every living creature on the earth and the living earth herself, too.

Seasoned Women just want to go on burning, burning, *blazing* across the whole of the sky in a red-hot spectacular eruption of fiery, passionate, caring, compassionate love for every living creature—right down to the end of our last spark and dying ember.

If the task of young adults is to create biological heirs, the task of old age is to create social heirs.
George Vaillant

Gallop Polls and University studies are now abounding with data that older people of all ages are much happier than their counterparts under 50. Theories cite many possible reasons: environmental, biological changes in brain and hormone chemistry, as well as an increase in the psychosocial traits of self-integration, self-esteem, and overall sense of well-being.[3]

Seasoned Women couldn't be happier: no more beauty contests, no more being judged by the size of our breasts, the firmness of our butts, or how many viable eggs we have left in our ovary sacs. We are thrilled that at last we are no longer defined by our jobs, professions, or by our relationships to our children or to our partner. We are downright giddy that at last we can speak our mind, take risks, step out of line, stray past the boundaries, and no longer feel the kind of gut-punching worries, stress, and fears that marked our younger years.

There's nothing left we need to prove to anyone else, except ourselves. Seasoned Women are thrilling at the challenge to leave a legacy of a happy and healthy future for *everyone's* children and grandchildren. We want there to be social heirs of our wisdom, sprinkling it far and wide to younger generations, letting an ambitious breeze pick it up and send it to every corner and continent around the entire world.

Our middles have grown round as earthen globes.

We have become vessels finely fired in life's kiln. For the first time ever in human history, the sheer number of Seasoned Women is significant and unprecedented. There are 40 million of us. 40 MILLION! Healthy, educated, diverse, socially and politically conscious. We are strong and sturdy enough to hold the whole world in our embrace, uniquely positioned to bring to bear enormous powers of influence within our families, and in local, national, and international affairs. To cradle a world roaming and ramming around like scared, orphaned adolescents, separated from their fellow humans, in anguish and torment, asleep in a collective nightmare. Out of rhythm. Out of balance. And out of options.

The Economic crisis. Depletion of our natural resources. Global warming. An imbalanced ecosystem. Pollution of the air, land and water. Extinction of animals and sea life. Disease. Hunger. Poverty. Overcrowding. Wars and conflicts over oil, land, water, religion, culture, identity.

Sacred Outrage

There are things that need protecting; there are things that need defending so that they can survive.

Just as we Seasoned Women have developed great capacities for gentle love and tender compassion, just as they have become rooted, grounded, and in rhythmic accord with the impulse of the universe, so too, have we developed a great *in*-ability to tolerate cruelty, violence, and harm; injustice, inequality, and unfairness.

It sickens our insides to see that our once-burgeoning planet has become such an inhospitable place for life. Everything that exists and lives and depends on air, land, and sea has been shoved down hard into a mighty struggle for survival—beaten down, beaten back, buried deep under the social, political, and economic inequities that have been inflicted by a vastly disproportionate few who are terribly misguided in values and vision.

We see what we see and we know what we know. And we are unable just to stand by idly while the world burns to the ground in madness, mayhem, and just-plain meanness; we cannot bear doing nothing when hearing so many agonized cries for help, terror-filled shrieks, and blood-curdling screams.

The Seasoned Woman, while gentle and loving, is also composed of equal heaping parts of pure iron will when it comes to fiercely defending that which needs defending and protecting what needs protecting.

When it comes to possessing the passion and the might and the ferocity to put a stop to the utterly unnecessary nonsense that has caused our world to run amok, one can best bet that it is Seasoned Women who are indeed, particularly and generously, well-endowed!

> It is part of a healthy instinctual psyche to have deep reactions to disrespect, threat, injury... a woman has the power, when provoked, to be angry in a mindful way— and that is powerful. Anger is one of her innate ways to begin to reach out to create and preserve the balances that she holds dear, all that she truly loves. It is both her

right and at certain times in certain circumstance a moral duty.

For women this means there is a time to reveal your incisors, your powerful ability to defend territory, to say, "This far and no farther, the buck stops here, and hold on to your hat, I've got something to say, this is definitely going to change.

The learning we are after is to know when to allow right anger and when not... knowing when to act in an integral manner.

Most of the time wolves avoid confrontation but when they must enforce territory, when something or someone constantly hounds them or corners them, they explode in their own powerful way. This happens rarely, but the ability to express this anger is in their repertoire and it should be within ours, too.

It is psychically sound for women to feel this anger. It is psychically sound for them to use this anger about injustice to invent ways to elicit useful change.

Collective rage is well utilized as motivation to seek out or offer support, to conceive of ways to impel groups or individuals into dialogue, or to demand accountability, progress, improvements.

These are proper processes in the pattern of women coming to consciousness, of their caring about what is essential and important to them.

We want to use anger as a creative force. We want to use it to change, develop and protect...

Right response carries insight and right amounts of compassion and strength mixed together.

There comes a time when it becomes imperative to release a rage that shakes the skies.

There is a time—even though these times are very rare, there is definitely a time—to loose all the fire power one has.

There is definitely a time for full-bore rage.

When women pay attention to the instinctual self, they know when it is time.

Intuitively
They know
and they act.
And it is right.
Right as rain.

Clarissa Pinkola Estés[4]

CHAPTER TWO

To Protect and Empower

When I was a grown woman with children of my own, my father and I would sit on his front porch in the high heat and humidity of central Florida, swatting at tickly gnats landing on our sticky necks. We would pop open salty shells of boiled peanuts and sip on cans of cold Budweiser while he told me about the America of his parents' era.

Born in Pennsylvania in 1927 to proud working-class German parents, my father was the youngest of seven children. His father, my grandfather, had supported them by working in the prosperous steel mills of Pittsburgh until The Depression hit.

In the years leading up to that fateful day in 1929 there had been an ever-widening economic gap growing. Wealth had become unevenly concentrated in the hands of a few corporate elites; corruption was the word of the day. Unholy alliances had been formed, nurtured, and protected between these elites and our nation's politicians. They had profited handsomely from making high-risk investments.

And finally the shiny bubble burst. The stock market came crashing down.

Investors of limited means saw their little nest eggs disappear. The middle class lost more and more of its purchasing power; workers were laid off; spending decreased further, leading to more layoffs. For those of more modest means, who had not invested in the stock markets, they saw what little money they had on paper virtually disappear into thin air as they went into their savings. The same was true for the well-off. On paper, their wealth also evaporated with the great crash of 1929.

The citizens of my grandparents' America became trapped under the grinding gears of a vicious cycle. Jobs were lost. Unemployment went through the roof. Hard-earned savings vanished. Investments were worthless. Homes were foreclosed on. Money was hoarded. Banks failed. For far too many, when it became impossible to take care of their families, they jumped out windows, plummeting to their deaths, allowing their families to cash in on their insurance policies.

If This Sounds Familiar, It Should. Keep Reading.

People were shaken to their cores, stunned, scared, desperate, in shock, grieving the loss of the American life that had been the festive atmosphere of the Roaring Twenties.

For many years, people staggered about under the economic crush caused by those elite wealthy few who had wrested power away from the many and then abused it for their own greed. They had helped themselves to the trust and economic well-being of hard-working and faithful Americans. The result was the abject ruination of countless human lives.

Year after year people stood in long bread lines and unending unemployment lines. They swarmed soup kitchens by day and huddled together in shanty towns at night located at the edges of towns, "homes" they had built out of various materials they'd salvaged and patched together: cardboard, tin, broken bricks, and boards.

People languished in distress. They looked to the federal government and the newly installed President Herbert Hoover for help, but Hoover did not believe that the primary job of a democratic government is to protect and empower its citizens.

From Bad to Worse

The economic crisis that had been visited upon them also brought with it a social crisis. Fear, desperation, and money problems weaken the joints of even the strongest of family structures. When it is prolonged and intractable, hearth and home, kith and kin, the ties that bind, become dry and brittle, frail and fragile. Knees buckled at kitchen sinks and upon the altars of every God. People and personalities become fractured along their fault lines.

Hopelessness, like a poison, oozed through veins and arteries, loosed upon tender hearts and exhausted minds, overlaying them with anxiety, depression, rage, dissociation, suicide, drug abuse, alcoholism, and domestic violence.

Sitting on the front porch with boiled peanuts and a cold Budweiser, I learned from my father that my prosperous German grandparents had lost everything in the Great Depression of a great nation, a country of hope and a haven to so many working immigrants. Their economic devastation led to their social devastation.

The evening dinner table became marred with rage exploding between my grandparents. Seven children ate their evening scraps to the yelling and screaming between my grandparents.

The Depression had unleashed a terror in them, but instead of placing blame on the rightful but faceless, corrupt corporate elite who had brought this economic and emotional disaster upon the whole nation, my grandmother instead harshly criticized the nearest person around, my grandfather, for having lost everything.

His response was to grab an enormous kitchen butcher knife, raise it high over his head and sink it deeply and angrily into the dining room table. Their seven children sat by trembling in trauma and stunned silence.

Protecting and Empowering Citizens

Sometimes you have to get angry to get things done.

Ang Lee

The America my father had grown up in had been jump-started by FDR. Within only 100 days of his election, through legislation and the exercising of his executive powers, FDR launched the New Deal, a variety of programs that began relieving unemployment and stimulating economic growth. He brought regulation to Wall Street, and to the banking and the transportation systems—all of these being the very ones who had crashed America.

Under FDR, living conditions improved rapidly. Manufacturing doubled. Employment returned. The economy grew.

There was a unifying of groups: labor unions, religious, ethnic and cultural minorities—Jews, Catholics, African Americans, marginalized groups, northerners, and rural southerners. Communities knitted themselves back together again in a spirit of "we're-all-in-this-together."

FDR had enabled Government to do what Government is supposed to do: protect and empower citizens.

Coming Full Circle

Protest and anger practically always derive from hope, and the shouting out against injustice is always in the hope of those injustices being somewhat corrected and a little more justice established.

John Burger

The America in which I came of age was not perfect. It was not always fair or just or equal. It was the late 60s, early 70s, with all its upheaval, people pouring into the streets protesting, bringing attention to a variety of social, political, and economic issues, calling for progressive values: equality for women, African Americans, minorities, and marginalized groups of people; an end to homelessness, poverty, oppression, crime, drug abuse; pleas and demands for the support of human rights everywhere; and justice for one and all.

I think all the clamor and chaos was our collective Humanity's way of trying to take some baby steps, however haltingly, however clumsily, in the direction of evolving ourselves as human beings into a higher, more developed, consciously aware place. In other words, working to raise the bar of what it means to be a human being! But the gallant efforts of so many courageous people to bring about the expansion of ourselves were met with resistance and a dumbfounding show of violence.

It always seems that light and darkness travel together. Good and Evil. Yin and Yang. The dance of opposites. In the 60s, America's baby steps forward found our bold visionary leaders gunned down in cold blood. JFK. MLK. Bobby Kennedy. Kent State students. By the time the 70s rolled up on us, there was a deep rupture in our American psyche and it cast a pall of stunned silence across our purple mountains' majesty.

The Similarities

The world needs anger. The world often continues to allow evil because it isn't angry enough.
Bede Jarrett

The policies FDR instituted were maintained throughout the many decades that followed, that is, until the late 70s, when America again began to be unraveled by the slow, insidious unfettering of the elite.

Every government administration since Reagan, including both Bushes, Clinton, and Obama, have undone the protective regulations put in place after the Great Depression which safeguarded and empowered citizens.

They have instead replaced them with harmful policies and legislation that benefit those corporate and special interest groups who have contributed obscene amounts to political candidates and their campaigns. Today it is the corporate and special interest groups who are crafting our bills and laws; the only role of our congressional and presidential representatives is to do their bidding.

And now what is happening again is that in our various forms of denial, distractions, addictions, and paralysis, the corporate elites and special interest groups have bought up our politicians, our media, our institutions, our votes, and are once again plundering the country, robbing us of our democracy.

The unraveling of America, again, is eerily similar to conditions leading up to the 1929 crash.

According to economist and former Labor Secretary, Robert Reich (2011), those parallels include:

• The income gap between the wealthy and the middle class. Just as in the Depression era, the gap is growing wider and wider.

• The drop in wages. As in the Depression, wages are also dropping and people found/find themselves having to spend more and go deeper into debt to maintain their standard of living.

• Economic Gains. In the 1920s, the economic gains that the country was making were not being circulated amongst the majority. Instead they were being shunted to the wealthy. Eighty years later, same story.

• A Casino Economy. Prior to the '29 crash, the rich folk whose incomes were soaring began gambling and speculating on a limited number of investments and assets.

Values blew through the roof. Just like balloons that are filled too much, they eventually POP! In the Depression, real-estate and stock bubbles burst! In 2007, after protective regulations and policies had been dismantled, the same sketchy real estate and bogus investments appeared. And then POPPED!

In 1928, Goldman Sachs had helped set up a crash with risky, albeit deliberate, speculations. In the crash of 1929, Goldman Sachs reaped the benefits of naïve investors.

In the 2000s, again Goldman Sachs created risky and deliberate speculations, and then in 2007, once again, as in the Great Depression, they cashed in on gullible homeowners and investors.

Like vultures, gleeful at the delicious stench of death, they gathered, swarmed, glided silently in wide circles through azure-blue skies, waiting, waiting, waiting to drop-pounce down on their juicy fresh road-kill.

As in 1929, Goldman Sachs again feasted royally after the 2007 crash.[5]

To Protect and Empower

The Differences.

There never was a social change in America without angry people at the heart.

Keith Miller

According to Reich (2011), in the years after 1929 citizens came together. They pulled together. They demanded that the government do what it is that government is supposed to do: protect and empower citizens. FDR listened and responded. Economic reforms and policies closed the gaping income divide and eliminated the economic hazards that had contributed to it. Programs were put in place to shore up the nation's infrastructure, its schools, and social safety. The middle class regained its strength and ability to be more "secure, prosperous and productive."

But that has not happened since 2007. The federal and state governments have been unresponsive to citizens. They are not protecting and empowering. They have not enacted policies, programs, or reforms that would eliminate the underlying causes of the bursting bubble. And worst of all, after the 2007 crash, citizens are not coming together and pulling together.[6]

I drive past unemployment offices. The lines are growing longer and longer. I drive by churches and missions. They cannot provide for the long lines of those who need food, rent, or electric bills paid.

Too many people are shaken to their cores, stunned, scared, desperate, in shock, grieving the loss of the American Dream they had been promised, that if one works hard and/or gets an education, one can create the foundation for living a meaningful life and achieving a prosperous future. More and more people are awakening with a thud from this national disillusionment. They are living the reality of a broken dream and the failed promise of our national social contract.

Just as in my grandparents' Depression era, people are once again staggering under the economic crush caused by those wealthy elite few who have wrested power away from the many and then abused it for their own greed. These elite few have helped themselves to the trust and economic well-being of hardworking and faithful Americans. The result is the same as for my grandparents, the abject ruination of countless human lives.

The concentration of income, wealth, and political power can be seen in the hands of Wall Street, pharmaceutical companies, the oil companies, big agribusiness, big insurance companies, military contractors, and rich individuals. The income gap widens. Unholy alliances have been formed, nurtured, and protected between these corporate elites and our nation's politicians. They have rigged the game in their favor. Profiting enormously from high-risk investments and the debt of citizens.

Banks gambled and lost. The government used citizens' tax money to bail them out and then neglected to impose regulations to see that it couldn't happen again. The craps-shoot plays on. The economy is crashing down. Jobs are lost. Homes are being foreclosed upon. Hard-earned savings have vanished. Investments are worthless. The middle class is losing more and more of its purchasing power.

Increasing numbers of lawyers, teachers, artists, and other professionals are unemployed or under-employed. So, too are our graduating college students finding themselves buried deep under student debt, unemployed, or under-employed.

Service workers, minimum-wage workers, civil service workers, health-care workers, domestic workers—many working a 40-hour week, are languishing at the poverty level, barely able to support themselves because wages are so low. They fall farther and farther below the poverty level as they gradually lose their ability to support themselves and their children.

In addition, there are fewer and fewer full time minimum-wage jobs available. Consequently, minimum-wage workers are not finding enough work to fill even a 40-hour week.

I think people should be angry at things that are worthy of anger. Injustice is outrageous and deserves anger.

Chris Hayes

I don't sit on the front porch with peanuts and beer and my father any more. He died in 2006, about one year before the bubble burst (again) and the economy collapsed (again). And now I find that there is the possibility that instead of leaving my children a country making progress in the direction of evolving ourselves as human beings, I run the risk of leaving them to languish in a looted, burned-out shell of a country, once a model to the world, that has lost its way, lost its founding values and principles.

Hard-working and well-meaning citizens are trapped in the grinding gears of a vicious cycle.

Pulitzer Prize winning journalist, Chris Hedges, sees it all so very clearly:

> The sooner we realize that we are locked in deadly warfare with our ruling, corporate elite, the sooner we will realize that these elites must be overthrown. The corporate oligarchs have now seized all institutional systems of power in the United States. Electoral politics, internal security, the judiciary, our universities, the arts and

finance, along with nearly all forms of communication, are in corporate hands.[7]

Unlike the 1920s or the 1960s, our usual methods for redressing imbalances and changing what needs to change are no longer available to us: elections, the media, the court system, they are now all bought up by the corporate elite and special-interest groups. Unions are dismantled. Universities, which are supposed to be environments of thought and discussion, now exist to pander to their donors and teach only their agenda.

This rigging of our political system and the economy is creating a social crisis as well. Fear, desperation, and money problems are weakening the joints of strong families. Hearth and home, kith and kin, the ties that bind, are becoming dry and brittle, frail and fragile. Knees are buckling at kitchen sinks and upon the altars of every God. Personalities are fracturing along fault lines. Hopelessness, like a poison, is oozing through veins and arteries, and is being loosed upon tender hearts and exhausted minds, overlaying them with ever-increasing rates of anxiety, depression, rage, dissociation, suicide, drug abuse, alcoholism, and domestic violence.

This realization shatters me: that we have faltered so egregiously when it comes to taking care of this precious gift we were entrusted with, of life and land and each other, that we are now threatened with our own extinction. A staggering thought! Terrifying and utterly heartbreaking!

"The seesaw of history has thrust the oligarchs once again into the sky," says Hedges. "We sit humiliated and broken on the ground. It is an old battle. It has been fought over and over again in human history. We never seem to learn. It is time to grab our pitchforks." Hedges says we have but one avenue open to us: revolt. A non-violent movement.[8]

Anger is a great force. If you control it, it can be transmuted into a power which can move the whole world.

William Shenstone

The time has come for Seasoned Women to mobilize Soulful Citizen Activists within their local communities to take sacred action.

Soulful Citizen Activists are those who come passionately alive in their communities, building relationships, networking, collaborating, communicating, and getting things done; weaving together the well-being of mates, children, families, workplaces, communities, and the environment; reorienting humans to our true and natural position in the world, and in the unfolding universe.

Come, come whoever you are!
Wanderer, Lover, Worshipper of fire,
It doesn't matter.
This is not a caravan of despair.
It is a portal of hope!
This is not the door of hopelessness
    and frustration.
It is a door open for everybody.
Come! Come as you are!

Rumi

Soulful Citizen Activists:
• Change institutions, attitudes and policies.
• Right wrongs, imbalances and injustices.
• Eliminate those influences that are detrimental or oppressive.
• Protect the rights and well-being of their fellow citizens.
• Commit to nonviolence.
• Are values-driven.

• Strive to transcend differences.
• Guide their community into making choices that up-hold the highest good of everyone.
• Oppose violence, cruelty, any kind of exploitation, or manipulation; greed; acts and attitudes of inhumanity that oppress people or strip them of their human dignity.
• Reject the abuse of power, calling instead for self-empowerment of the people.
• Realize that the responsibility for bringing about real and lasting change depends on citizens coming together to make it happen, not leaving it to the government, political systems or corporations.

Come, come whoever you are!

CHAPTER THREE

Unplugging the Power Sources

Gene Sharp is old now, his once-great mane of hair has thinned like kite string against his scalp. His speech is slowed, a bit slurred; his eyes are clouded, watering, and crusty. He is bent, stooped, frail, and fragile. Dressed in brown Hush Puppies and an olive green corduroy jacket, he hobbles with a cane around his Boston office at the Albert Einstein Institution where these days he is working harder than ever. On the phone. On his computer. Still writing, still speaking, still teaching, still giving advice to a world hungry for what he has to offer.

For 40 years Professor Sharp has studied and written about the nature and potential of nonviolent revolutions. He is the go-to guy, for the whole world, for citizens who have had enough and want to rid themselves of oppressive, life-threatening governments. Dr. Sharp wrote a small pocket book entitled *From Dictatorship to Democracy,* which has been translated into over 30 languages and used on every continent except Antarctica. Like manna falling from on high, citizens' groups have used his guide to design strategies to topple their ruling regimes.

According to Dr. Sharp, creating a society built on freedom and peace requires four things, starting with strategic skills, organization, and planning. The fourth element is perhaps the most important to understand. And that is **POWER**. Citizens who wish to create change must not only bear in mind, but take it into their heart, that the most crucial tool at their disposal is **their ability to apply their own POWER to achieve their goals.**

But what is this power and how is it applied?

Dr. Sharp tells us that for governments to be able to hold power over citizens what is needed is the assistance, cooperation, submission, and the obedience of—can you guess?—of *the citizens*.

Governments are able to maintain this hold over us by use of:

• *Authority,* that is, people believing that they have a moral duty to obey their government.

• *Human Resources,* that is, the sheer numbers of people who assist, cooperate, submit, and obey.

• *Skills and Knowledge,* that is, those obedient people supplying the regime with skills and knowledge so that they can perform specific actions to keep the masses under control.

• *Intangible factors,* that is, using psychological or ideological propaganda to induce people to continue to obey and to assist the rulers.

• *Material Resources,* that is, the extent to which the rulers control property, natural resources, financial resources, and the economic, communication, and transportation systems.

• *Sanctions,* that is, threatening or applying punishments to those who are disobedient as an incentive to fall back in line.[9]

When citizens are obedient, this simply increases the sources of government power. Conversely, to decrease the government's hold, citizens need only to unplug the government's power sources (those sources listed above). Without those supporting power sources, the overlords of the people see their powers diminish and ultimately dissolve. Governments and regimes depend on the cooperation, submission, and obedience of the citizens; without it, over time, the ability to keep a muddy boot on the necks of citizens ceases to exist.

(Interestingly enough, Sharp tells us that, as it turns out, the good news is that when such governments impose sanctions, punishments, and threats on citizens, that is not sufficient to cause citizens to return to a necessary degree of obedience and submission.)

Given enough time for the elites to experience a good, strong power outage, they eventually become impotent, lapsing into paralysis.

Then comes disintegration.

Then comes political starvation.

Then comes the death of the power regime.

According to Dr. Sharp—and this is a crucial point, "the degree of liberty or tyranny in any government is, it follows, in large degree a reflection of the relative determination of the subjects to be free and their willingness and ability to resist efforts to enslave them."[10]

> *The degree of liberty*
> *is a reflection*
> *of the determination*
> *of the subjects*
> *to be free*
> *and their willingness*
> *and ability*
> *to resist efforts to enslave them.*

CHAPTER FOUR

LOST
Desolate and lone
All night long on the lake
Where fog trails and mist creeps,
The whistle of a boat
Calls and cries unendingly,
Like some lost child
In tears and trouble
Hunting the harbor's breast
And the harbor's eyes.

Carl Sandburg

It's not rocket science; it's common sense.

Research is now telling us what Seasoned Women have known all along:

That it is cooperation, not competition, that has allowed human beings to survive and flourish.

There are many sound studies coming out now that are confirming what Seasoned Women have already grown wise in realizing:

That no matter how far back one thinks the origins of human history stretch, if competition among humans is the overwhelming and prevailing nature of human beings; and if violence, war, and conflict are our overriding intrinsic traits for solving problems, then we would have wiped our silly selves off the planet long ago!

The fact that humans are still inhabiting the earth is testament to the truth that we have taken care of each other far, far more than we have killed each other off.

Across every social, biological, economic, and ecological discipline, research and practitioners alike are all reaching the same conclusions about our *real* inborn and dominant trait being that of cooperation. And yet these findings will not be enough to loosen the grip of the utter nonsense that has been pumped into us about who we are as humans.

It is only in our very recent history that we have been filled with delusions about our core natures being that of rugged individualists and a survival of the fittest. A lone wolf going it alone. Only in our recent history have we been misled about how we should prize acquisitiveness over stewardship, almighty profit over the welfare of people, and to value competition over cooperation.

We have been indoctrinated to believe that there is some absurd admonition coming from somebody's absurd interpretation of somebody's almighty god who has given the thumbs-up blessing and a holy high-five for corporations and governments to go forth, conquer, subdue, and have dominion over every person and every creature of every land, every sea, and the unlimited sky, free to ravage the earth and plunder its people, on a never-ending blood-thirsty mission for power and profit, turning everything and everyone into a commodity that can be bought and sold in their own rigged market.

Those who seek to commandeer the world for themselves and for their own exclusive benefit have lost their way as human beings. And they are dragging us down with them. They have become separated from themselves, from others, and from our natural place within the earth system and in the greater universe. And they are forcing this upon the rest of us.

They are marauding through our streets, trampling us over with greed and oppression, drugging us with perverse falsehoods and cunningly sly nonsense about what it means to be a human being: claiming that all of us should aspire to claw our way to some mythical top of some mountain-heap, climbing over dead bodies on the way up, in a drive to be the biggest, the best, have the most toys, to wield the most power, in some massive orgy of excess and phantasmagoric splendor. And we capitulate.

What we are being told to believe about ourselves as humans is grotesquely incorrect, dangerously misleading, and deeply false. It has brought us squarely and unequivocally to the point of facing a massive conglomeration of converging disasters.

As I'm traveling around, I meet small children. And when I look at a small child and think how we've harmed this beautiful planet since I was that age, I feel a kind of desperation, anger and shame.

Jane Goodall

Only in the last 100 years have we come to know that humans are the latest iteration of a 13-*BILLION*-year-old evolutionary longing to bring forth ever-more dynamic and complex forms of life. Only in our recent history have we come to know that our ancestral descent is an unbroken link of life, diverse and fiercely determined, in a vast and stupendous universal feat of divine creation. A process that is so much larger than any of us could possibly, completely conceive.

And only in recent history, in the past 100 years, have humans managed to create so many global disasters, of such profoundly dangerous magnitude, that our human species, plant and animal life, and even the earth itself, is threatened with annihilation.

Lost

It took the universe 13 billion years to evolve us here onto this earth within a delicate and intricate system of interconnection and interdependence, existing in balance to everything and everyone else.

We have evolved stunningly magnificent bodies, brains, hearts, and spirits, and with these extraordinary gifts, have been tasked with the responsibility of making sure that we do our part to live within the system and to protect the conditions under which Life can go on blazing forth in brilliant flourish.

Yet! Within a mere 100 years, with great arrogance we have managed to interfere so seriously with the mechanics of ourselves and every living system that we are at the point of destroying it all.

We are living outside the natural order of who we really are as human beings and what our true place and purpose is. We dishonor the mystery of life and creation, and of the Creator. We have squandered the sacred gifts bequeathed to us: bodies, brains, hearts, and spirits.

Seasoned Women have long known what research and practitioners are now telling us, that we are now living in a world that has been built on an unsustainable model, a house of cards. The scientists and the experts, in all their learned knowledge, will not save us. If we wish to survive and leave a healthy, sustainable planet to our grandchildren, if we wish to do our part to maintain an intact chain of burgeoning life, then Seasoned Women everywhere urgently need to step up and step forward into roles as leaders and guides, to bring people together into a discussion about who we are as humans and how we show up in the world. Seasoned Women need to step up and step forward to reframe the conversation about who we are as humans in context with our 13-billion-year-old legacy.

I think, for one, we have to really accept that anger is a normal human emotion that can be a positive force for change.

Koren Zailckas

There's a new way of being in the world that is trying to take shape and form, one in which the welfare of the earth, with all its myriad life forms, becomes the continuous and conscious focus and choice. There is a new world trying so very hard to emerge, to be born, and Seasoned Women are needed to midwife it into being.

Seasoned Women know this. We get it. We have our minds and hearts wrapped around the problem. We have a clear brain, sharpened senses, and a keen eye. We see through the trailing fog and creeping mist.

We are shattered and heartbroken by the world's suffering, by the calls and cries of all who are lost. All of us are in tears and trouble.

In a divine balance of fierceness and tenderness, in boldness and in service, we Seasoned Women are being called to tend the world.

It is a lack of balance that has brought us precisely to this momentous time in our history. A time of crisis. And a time of exciting opportunity. A time to create new models to take us into the next era of our evolving human nature. A time to create new relationships between the masculine and feminine energies and influence. A time to acknowledge the bridge between Science and Spirit. A time to create economic systems based on compassion, fairness, and sustainability. A time to reorient and adapt ourselves within the ecological earth and life systems upon which we depend utterly for our survival.

We need to question and to re-define our premises about who we are.

Lost

We need to re-tool our mindset about what it means to live together, in relationship to everything else.

Anger is a good motivator.

James Dyson

Unfortunately the gathering of hard facts and the presenting of indisputable figures, across the expanse of social, political, economic, and ecologic tracts, is not going to be enough to halt current destructive practices and policies, or to dissuade the hearts and minds of those who believe they are entitled to help themselves to the world's resources and endanger the well-being of human psyches and souls. They will not magically come around to seeing the errors of their ways.

What is needed is to create a vision for the future that wholly encompasses the designing of communities, nations, and a world that will benefit the many, not just an elite few.

America was founded on a vision of freedom, and a particular set of values and principles. Since its founding, those who have stepped forward and fought valiantly, campaigned tirelessly, and suffered greatly to build upon, expand, uphold, maintain, and pass along our vision, values, and principles, have included women, African Americans, immigrants, laborers, abolitionists, Native Americans, homosexuals, and those from every other marginalized group we can recall or imagine, along with those relativley rare individuals whose values dictated that they act for the welfare of others, rather from their own self-defined interests.

It is by their life's work that America's values and principles have endured, evolved, grown, and are now at a juncture that they must urgently expand.

Our vision, values, and principles have been passed from one generation to the next and abide deep inside the American psyche and collective soul.

On November 19, 1863, President Abraham Lincoln stood on the battlefield of Gettysburg and left us an address that is as relevant today as it was then:

...It is for us the living, rather, to be dedicated here to the unfinished work which they who fought here have thus far so nobly advanced. It is rather for us to be here dedicated to the great task remaining before us—that from these honored dead we take increased devotion to that cause for which they gave the last full measure of devotion—that we here highly resolve that these dead shall not have died in vain—that this nation, under God, shall have a new birth of freedom—and that government of the people, by the people, for the people, shall not perish from the earth.

But something has gone terribly wrong. Once again we find ourselves in fear, desperation, money problems. with family joints weakened. Hearth, home, kith and kin, the ties that bind, becoming dry and brittle, frail and fragile. Knees buckling at kitchen sinks and upon the altars of every God. People and personalities fracturing along fault lines. Hopelessness loosed. Tender hearts and exhausted minds overlain with anxiety, depression, rage, dissociation, suicide, drug abuse, alcoholism, and domestic violence.

Usually when people are sad, they don't do anything. They just cry over their condition. But when they get angry, they bring about a change.
James Russell Lowell

Lost

All of us are here, right now, in this place, at this time, experiencing the burning of the world and we are being called to burn, burn, BURN with passionate soulful action to set right a nation that has careened off in the wrong direction.

Our Values and Principles

Seasoned Women know that to have an optimally-functioning, fully-contributing society, all of its members need to be contributing their magnificent and diverse talents, skills, abilities, and gifts.

In order for that to happen, the citizenry needs to be educated, healthy, and operating with a decent standard of living. This is not rocket science, and facts and figures will not save us; but our values will:

Cognitive scientist, George Lakoff, lays out clearly, simply, and succinctly the American values we hold dear:

• Being **protected** from the economic threat and duress of corporate corruption.

• Being freed up to live **meaningful lives;** and wishing the same for everyone.

• Having **opportunities** to explore and create what it means to have a meaningful life.

• Establishing **fairness** and **equality** as crucial in supporting our innate human compassion and need for freedom.

• Understanding that food, shelter, education, and good health are valued as a **necessary foundation** to creating a meaningful life, and that in order to create this foundation, working and earning a certain **base income** is required.

• Understanding that the value of **community** has been hard won and painfully realized; that nobody makes it alone. When it comes to creating and living a fulfilling life, we need each other.[11]

All of our history, including The Great Depression, has taught us how much power citizens hold when they come together and work together to rid themselves of villains who try to help themselves to greed and power at the expense of the common good. It is not facts and figures that will save us, but as Lakoff reminds us, our cherished American principles will.

1. The **Common Good** Principle. Individuals contributing to the overall common good which multiplies its benefit back to individuals by providing:
• *Protection,* through police, firefighters, military and court system.
• *Fulfillment in life* and *opportunities,* through schools, universities, national parks, roads, a banking system to start a business.
• *Freedoms,* including *freedom from want,* as established by the Constitution and the Bill of Rights, safeguarded by the courts.
• *Fairness* and *equality,* working to eliminate discrimination and uneven standards.
• *Prosperity* through *community,* no one is an island; we are all in this together. We rise together; we fall together.
• *Preserving our shared resources,* that serve all of us, preserving national parks, beaches, oceans, rivers, streams, the electromagnetic spectrum (giving us radio, TV, other forms of communication), the Internet, our scientific knowledge, and genetic heritage.

2. The **Expansion of Freedom** Principle always leads Americans to evolve fundamental civil liberties such as voting, civil and working rights; public education and health and consumer protection.

3. The **Human Dignity** Principle calls us to stand in our compassion and responsibility as a country and

decide where the boundaries of human dignity fall with regard to the basics of food, shelter, education and health care.

4. The **Diversity** Principle recognizes that including a broad range of elements, whether in decision-making or in families, workplaces, schools, communities or nations fosters rich complexity that allows for greater success, a stronger foundation, increased opportunities and more meaningful and fulfilling lives for the many, and not just a few.[12]

We Seasoned Women are the bearers of life, here now to midwife the birth of a new world and to help us remember who we are as human beings and why we are here.

Lost, desolate and lone, we hear the whistle of the boat and the calls and cries unendingly.

It is we Seasoned Women who are the harbor's breast and the harbor's eyes.

CHAPTER FIVE

The Answer

My ninth-grade civics teacher was a tiny little woman in spiked high heels with a huge personality that gushed with energy, fun, and enthusiasm. And while my 14-year-old head was filled with thoughts of cute boys, Friday-night football games, slumber parties, and lunch, my brain somehow managed to absorb that the United States is divided up into states; states are divided up into counties; counties are divided up into smaller units of incorporated or unincorporated cities, towns, townships, villages, hamlets, and municipalities.

Within these smaller communities of cities, towns, townships, villages, hamlets, and municipalities, citizens elect local citizens to pass local laws. They exercise influence and a degree of autonomy and self-governance. Local citizens make local decisions about what kind of community they want to live in and what kind of community they want to create together.

Of Mastodons and Men

At the heart of every tale about human survival and evolution is the story of community. Groups of people coming together; banding together; relying on each other; realizing that they can accomplish so much more when working together; increasing their supplies and resources by utilizing the unique contribution of each of its members.

We've come far since our Nomadic ancestors figured out how to take hunting small game and gathering forest tidbits to a whole other level. At some point, they talked among themselves and developed a vision of bringing down a mighty mastodon, which meant more food for all, more protein, and meant they wouldn't have to work so hard and so often at securing the lighter fare of little rabbits and tiny berries.

But bagging a mastodon required the collective action of the community, an action plan and the co-operation of its members.

The rest, as they say, is history. From the time of the hunters and gatherers, the idea and practice of community caught on, proliferated across every land and nation, evolving into even greater forms of complexity, and continues today to draw upon those same principles of collective action and cooperation.

The Nature of Nature

Today the community continues to be the primary powerhouse when it comes to creating a vision of a better life. Communities continue to carry the greatest potential for bringing change where change is needed. Communities are members banding together in collective action, each bringing their unique contributions.

Communities continue to possess enough potential fierceness to ward off danger from all the wild things, like corporate and political animals who are roaming loose across every mountain, desert, and savanna, wreaking havoc on the common good; harming people of every nation who are only trying to survive and care for themselves and their families.

As it turns out, communities come together and operate in the exact same image and likeness as that of the overall universe, copying the very template used by the universe in its design for creating diverse and complex lifeforms. It is a systems approach. The universe is a system comprised of a multitude of interrelated, interconnected, and interdependent systems.

So, too, are communities, a system comprised of interrelated, interconnected, and interdependent systems.

The simplest definition of a system is that it is a set of interrelated components, acting with a common purpose, that exchanges information and energy with its environment.

This could apply equally to a home heating system (mechanical), the body's digestive system (biological), Calculus (mathematical), the solar system (astronomical), nuclear fission (chemical), existentialism (philosophy), the Cold War (political), or a family (social).

Diamond and McDonald[13]

All these systems have the same general characteristics:
• A purpose or primary task,
• Constituent parts that are simultaneously whole systems in themselves and subsystems of the larger whole,
• Activities, that affect the energy and information coming into the system so that they leave in a different state,
• Boundaries that manage those exchanges and structures that organize those activities,
• Some means of self-regulation and adaptation that allow them to change over time, with changing conditions and an environment or an even larger supra-

system, which provides the context within which they operate.

Diamond and McDonald[14]

That Extra Something

While the universe was unfolding its lavish creation of human beings, and nestling them inside a social system, there is something extra that has been developing over time: *Consciousness*.

Following Diamond and McDonald, human beings have

> the ability to actively and intentionally participate in the functioning and organization of the system. It is this consciousness that makes human systems so infinitely exciting and complex and so useful and appropriate to study.
>
> It is the intentionality of our individual and collective human behavior that shapes our social, political and economic realities on this planet. How we think, what we value, what we believe, what we want and need, and what we choose to pursue determine how we organize our community, national, international and transnational lives.
>
> In short, these factors create the world we live in, now and in the future.

Diamond and McDonald[15]

All things are connected. Whatever befalls the earth befalls the sons of the earth. Man does not weave the web of life; he is merely a strand of it. Whatever he does to the web, he does to himself.

Ted Perry

Communities today have evolved into complex systems with interrelating, interconnecting, interdependent, and overlapping parts that include:
• Government
• Nongovernmental Organizations
• Business and Commerce
• Education and Research
• Religion
• Media and Communication
• Funding Streams
• Citizen Activists
• The Arts

Each of these separate parts, taken together, build the structure—the framework—upon which communities raise themselves.

Each of these civil sector parts, combined, contribute to the whole, creating a community system whose sole purpose and aim is to enable its members to live in an optimal environment in which they are able to maximize their gifts, talents, skills, and abilities. Taken together, these interrelated, interconnecting, interdependent, and overlapping civil sectors build the foundation upon which communities and their citizen members should be able to live in optimal health, prosperity and contribution.

When it comes to building community and creating the best, deepest, and most long-lasting outcomes, each of these parts in the system is not only crucial to the whole, but each is equal in importance. As in all systems, it becomes necessary simultaneously to include and develop each part alongside all the other parts of the system.

Whatever He Does to the Web, He Does to Himself...

The Answer

The impulse of the universe is passed on through all of us, absolutely genetically wired into our very DNA, to go on creating the best environment in which our communities can support the passionate longing of Life to go on creating more Life. As humans, we come endowed with the conscious ability to make intentional choices that insure success, the same duplicating mechanism by which the universe operates. Cooperation, connection, balance.

Conversely, we are now also experiencing the human capacity to use consciousness to make destructive choices, choices that are bringing about the destruction of the earth as well as our own extinction, through competition, separation, and imbalance.

Communities are wounded, struggling to feed families; its members, unemployed, underemployed, overcome with fear, anger, sadness, despair, working and working and working, and yet being stampeded by corporate and political mastodons who have used their might to rig the big game against us.

The civil sectors of American society: government, NGOs (non-governmental organizations), businesses, educational organizations, faith communities, the media, the arts, individual and other funders, and activists have currently been seized by those with an agenda that is dangerously antithetical to what is trying to emerge in the greater community of human beings. The world is in a powerful pull between forces that would give it life and those that would take it away.

We face critical global challenges that require urgent and innovative solutions. We are living in a time when the worst thing that has ever happened on earth is happening now and it is humans who have caused:
• The economic crisis
• The exhaustion of our natural resources

- Global warming
- The dangerous imbalance of our ecosystem
- The pollution of our air, land and water
- The extinction of animals and sea life
- Disease
- Hunger
- Overcrowding
- Wars, conflict, and fighting over
    - Oil
    - Land
    - Water
    - Religion
    - Culture
    - Identity
- A maladaptive lifestyle and belief system resulting in unrestrained materialism
- Aggression, as valued over peaceful coexistence; competition, as prized over cooperation; and acquisitiveness, as eclipsing our being good stewards of the planet.

Our Birthright and Our Mandate

All around the globe, the core traits that are truly human, those of compassion, cooperation, and a longing for healthy and meaningful connections through relationships and community are pulsing inside so many people. So many are bursting with fierce passion to get out from underneath antiquated and outdated ideas and to contribute instead to creating a world in which human beings can be authentic and genuinely human.

So many are enthusiastically embracing our advances in knowledge, technology and spirituality. They are hopping, skipping, and joyfully jumping to advance into higher states of human awareness and what it actually means to be an alive and an evolving human inside a magnificent system of such mysterious and profoundly loving fecundity. They want desperately to contribute to the ongoing success of an evolving universe by cooperating with, and participating in, its Divine Order, in order to create the optimal conditions for life by reaching inside ourselves and outwards towards each other for our best, highest, and deepest experiences.

Living as systems of compassionate, connected, cooperative, and balanced beings within our greater universal system that so ecstatically celebrates life in all of its varieties, combinations and quantities, is not only our birthright; it is our mandate.

It is Seasoned Women who can, and must, help the world to claim it. With every ounce of determination and insistence. Against all odds, counterforces and prevailing powerful pushbacks.

The Answer

The answer to an ailing nation lies in strong communities, communities that are integrated and operating for the economic, health, education, and welfare of all its members, not just an elite few. The way to go around the counterforces and the obstructions is by building strong communities using practical steps, concrete tools, and the ancient soul wisdom of connection and cooperation.

Long before our present iteration of humans burst onto this earth, our ancestors had figured out that community is the answer for protection and empowerment, that our well-being is tied to that of others, that maximizing the contribution and highest potential of all members not only increases the quality of life for all, but which, as it turns out, is ultimately in our own best interest.

Communities are created from out of our innate human natures of cooperation and connection, and in the process, our compassion for others is set happily free. It is why we care about human rights and fairness and equality. As Lakoff expressed this:

> We care about protecting our people in all ways, from criminals, fire, disease, disasters, impure food, dangerous working conditions, consumer fraud, and poverty in old age.
>
> It is why we care about empowerment of both individuals and businesses: roads and bridges for transportation, the Internet and satellites for communication, public schools for education, a banking system for capital, a court system for contracts.
>
> It is why we care about checks and balances against authoritarian power. It is why we place that care in a Government we choose.
>
> Empathy is also at the heart of ecological consciousness. It transcends political parties and national boundaries. Our connection to the natural world and to other beings is central to our humanity.
>
> Lakoff[16]

Fierce in Heart and Full of Soul

Community is the answer to an ailing nation. And Seasoned Women are the answer to community.

Seasoned Women know how to let go of old and unsustainable patterns and fixed positions and to embrace common ground, similarities, shared values, mutual goals and sustainable practices.

Seasoned Women know how to live inside a system of systems. They understand that deep and lasting change comes when the civil sectors of society's web of interconnecting parts operate together for a common goal.

Seasoned Women know how to raise awareness, educate, inform, and enable others to engage, connect, organize, and take mutual and ongoing action towards solving challenges.

Seasoned Women know how to find solutions that foster inclusion and interactive relationships and incorporate the input of all its members.

Seasoned Women know how to bring people together, to join with Soulful Citizen Activists of all ages, to dream a new collective vision for ourselves, to create a plan of action and intention for how to create a commonwealth in which members can have a foundation for developing to their utmost, contributing their unique qualities, skills, and abilities towards theirs, and others', ongoing material and spiritual prosperity.

They know our best chance to pull back from the brink of destruction calls for communities to come together, band together and work together to secure the conditions necessary for insuring the health, education and well-being of all its members so that they can contribute fully to the flourishing of their community.

Working across all sectors and within various groups, Seasoned Women, who are fierce in heart and full of soul, are the key to rebuilding a nation, community by community. Starting locally and working collectively with others. Community by community, the result will be a nation, and a world, balanced, in harmony, in peace, and in prosperity.

CHAPTER SIX

Core Issues

Throughout the United States there are many urgent challenges that are demanding our immediate attention.

In the fall of 2010 many earnest people from various walks, from all across America, who cared very deeply about doing something about the many wrong directions the country has taken, came together in Freedom Plaza in Washington D.C. This diverse group of citizens compiled a list of fifteen core crises that are currently facing the U.S.

These issues drive to the very heart of what it means to live in a land that extols freedom and democracy. These 15 issues are the foundation upon which this nation must balance itself.

Seasoned Women are being called to step forward into leadership roles and to mobilize others into soulful citizen action to solve these challenges and rectify these crises. It means that we are consciously, and with a most deliberate intention, contributing to the ongoing evolution of this nation, a dynamic system of interrelating and interconnecting parts whose preordained, ongoing mission is to be creating ever-new ways of being inclusive, expansive, creative, and compassionate.

In poll after poll after poll, citizens are expressing a groundswell of majority support for finding solutions that put the rights and needs of the people and the planet before the greedy grabbiness of ruthless corporations and their puppet politicians who have deafened their ears to the voice of the people.

Here are those Fifteen Core Issues that Seasoned Women can help the country to face and then work together with Soulful Citizen Activists to find solutions:

1. Corporatism. Firmly establish that money is not speech, corporations are not people, and only people have Constitutional rights. End corporate influence over the political process. End corporate welfare that enriches the few and instead begin treating government investment as something that all profit from. Ensure corporations pay their fair share by ending corporate loopholes and tax subsidies and put in place a global tax so that offshoring of money does not avoid taxes. Protect people and the environment from damage by corporations and end corporate trade agreements and partnerships that undermine consumer, labor, and environmental protections.

2. Wars and Militarism. End wars and occupations, end private for-profit military contractors and end the weapons-export industry. War crimes, crimes against humanity, and crimes against peace must be addressed and those responsible held accountable under international law. Reduce the national security state and demilitarize the police.

3. Human Rights. End exploitation of people in the US and abroad. End discrimination in all forms (race, gender, sexual orientation, and ethnicity), guarantee equal civil rights, and the right of people to travel across borders to work and live. Make the Universal Declaration of Human Rights a reality.

4. Worker Rights and Jobs. Guarantee that all working-age people have the right to safe, just, non-discriminatory, and dignified working conditions, a sustainable living wage, paid leave and economic protection. Put in place policies that allow worker-owned and -managed businesses, such as worker-owned cooperatives, and that allow for its workers to be able to build wealth and have greater control over their economic lives.

5. Government. Guarantee that all processes of the three branches of government are accountable to international law, transparent, and following the rule of law. Respect the civil rights of government employees. Create a work environment in government that encourages service to people, honesty, integrity, and participation in civil service, including protection for whistleblowers. Build policies and infrastructure that allow people to participate in decision-making.

6. Elections. Guarantee that all citizens 18 and older have the right to vote without barriers. Establish a universal voter registration. Guarantee that all candidates have the right to be heard in open debates and to run with low-threshold ballot-access laws. Count all votes in a transparent method open to the public. Institute new voting systems so that more than majority views are represented and so that voting systems can avoid voting based on fear of the greater evil; this could involve instant runoff or ranked-choice voting. Create a level playing-field by funding public elections with public dollars and clean election laws. Require that all donations directly and indirectly to elections should be transparent, i.e., no anonymous funding of elections.

7. Criminal Justice and Prisons. End stop-and-frisk and other racial-profiling police-practices that lead to police harassment, brutality, and even killings of civilians. Respect constitutional rights against search and seizure, as well as the right to counsel and against self-incrimination. End the drug war and adopt a public-health, evidence-based, drug policy that respects individual rights and does not rely on law enforcement. End private for-profit prisons and mandatory sentencing. Recognize the right of prisoners to humane and just conditions with a focus on rehabilitation and reintegration into society. Abolish the death penalty. Police need to protect the right to peaceably assembly to redress grievances, and the right to Freedom of Speech without infiltration or other police practices that undermine those rights.

8. Healthcare. Create a national, universal comprehensive health system that is publicly funded. Promote wellness in public policy. Recognize that health is a human right not a commodity.

9. Education. Guarantee that all people have the right to a high quality, publicly-funded, broad education from pre-school through vocational training or university.

10. Housing. Guarantee that all people have the right to affordable and safe housing. End predatory mortgage and foreclosure practices.

11. Environment. Adopt policies which effectively create a carbon-free and nuclear-free energy economy, one that respects the rights of nature. Confront climate change with a rapid and comprehensive transition to an energy-efficient, wind, solar and other renewable source-based economy that ends the wasteful use of energy. End the extractive economy and move toward a circular system where there is no waste and everything is reused. Remake land-use planning to support a healthy environment.

12. Finance and the Economy. Break up the too-big-to-fail banks. Develop public banks in every state and major city. Encourage community banks and credit unions. Create local stock exchanges to allow investment in local communities and create microfinance loans to encourage entrepreneurship and support local businesses. Remake the Federal Reserve into a transparent, democratic institution that responds to the needs of the economy and not to the needs of big banks. Put limits on the discrepancy between worker and executive pay. End policies which foster a wealth divide and move to a localized and democratic financial system. Guarantee that people's deposits are protected and that the public does not pay for financial institutions that fail. Reform taxes so that they are progressive and provide goods, monetary gain, and services for the people, including creating a guaranteed national income.

13. Media. End the concentration of media by a small number of corporations. Democratize the media by recognizing that the airwaves and the internet are public goods and recognize independent and citizen's media as legitimate media outlets. Require that media be accurate and accountable to the people and that the internet be accessible to all people. Respect people's privacy and promote the sharing of information.

14. Food and Water. Create systems that protect the land and water. Create local, affordable, and sustainable food networks. Encourage community-supported agriculture and farmer's markets and diversify local food supplies so that food does not depend on transit over long distances. Encourage organic food production free of chemicals and end genetically modified foods. Guarantee the right to produce and harvest seeds. Stop commodification of water and guarantee access to water as a public good.

15. Transportation. Provide affordable, clean, and convenient public transportation and safe spaces for pedestrian and non-automobile travel. Develop land-use planning that creates communities that are pedestrian- and bicycle-friendly (that are walkable and bikeable), with mass transit so that people do not depend on automobiles. Improve travel by train, rapid transit, and commuter rails, so people are not dependent on air travel and automobiles.[17]

CHAPTER SEVEN

NEVER DOUBT

That a large group
Of thoughtful committed Seasoned Women
Can change the world;
Indeed,
It may be the only thing that can.

I once lived in a county with one of the highest pregnancy rates in the nation. Girls were getting pregnant between three and six o'clock in the afternoon. The high school dropout rate was alarming. Poverty was soaring. Too many kids had no health-care coverage. Too many were bumping around in the streets after school with no supervision. The list went on.

One evening after dinner, my kids were outside playing, squeezing every last bit of light out of the day before coming inside to homework and baths. I flipped on the news. There came a story from Philadelphia about the five living presidents (Clinton, Carter, Ford, Bush, Sr. and Reagan, represented by wife Nancy) coming together to launch a new initiative called America's Promise. Retired General Colin Powell was to be the chairperson. Delegates from all over the U.S. were attending the week-long summit.

The initiative was founded on the vision and mission of providing our children with a foundation that would enable them to be healthy and successful, a foundation consisting of five essential needs: a healthy start, caring adults, a good education, safe places to be after school, and a way to give back to their communities.

At no time in the history of the U.S. had five living presidents ever come together for anything! Irrespective of their political parties, they stood shoulder to shoulder, waving, smiling, cheering, encouraging the delegates to go back into their communities and start local initiatives that would address these five critical needs.

I sat watching the screen and thinking what an incredibly remarkable and worthy endeavor it was. I sat there thinking how much the kids in my county could benefit from such an initiative. For the next five evenings, I followed the news coverage coming out of Philadelphia, paying close attention to see if there was a delegate attending from my county, but there was not. By the end of the week, I had managed to find the name and contact information for the delegate who was attending from the next county over. He was an executive with the local YMCA and by the time Monday morning rolled around and he got his feet back up under his desk, I had him on the phone filling his ear with my excitement about the initiative and my sadness over the fact that no delegate had been there from my county.

So start one yourself, he said. What? Me? Start a local America's Promise initiative? Why not? he said. Well, I said, I never have and I don't know how. Call your United Way, he said, and ask them to help.

I hung up and thought about it. It seemed like such a daunting undertaking. Surely I wasn't smart enough, I told myself. And I don't have the right credentials, I said. Who would listen to me, I wondered? And then I thought about the numbers of kids in my county who were languishing without the essentials, doomed to a meager and marginal life.

So with knees knocking and voice stammering, I picked up the phone, dialed the United Way and made an appointment to meet with the person in charge of community initiatives. I gathered together information about the launch of America's Promise and the grim statistics about the kids in the county. We met and I sat across the desk giving my best pitch for why a local initiative should be pursued. I was braced for any and all objections. I was ready with my responses to counter any and all rejections. Wide-eyed, white-knuckled and a mouth full of cotton, I finished my presentation. I stared across the desk at the director and was totally dumbfounded when he replied, "Sure! Sounds great! Why don't you spearhead it? The United Way will provide you with help, support and resources. We can make it a three-year project."

Just like that, I was thrust into the role of making it happen.

I called up four people I thought would care about it, too. We met over coffee. They each knew other people who would want to get involved and called them up. We met again with our ever-widening circle. More and more people were contacted and interested in getting involved. Our meeting places expanded from a coffee shop to a meeting room at the United Way, to a meeting room at the library, and then to a large student cafeteria at a local high school.

By the time we reached 120 people we divided up into committees. One of the first things we did was to begin compiling and gathering together information about who was in the community: who were the people, which were the public and private organizations, associations, and institutions. These, I learned, are the basic building blocks and they are the driving power source for creating a successful community.

Part One: Discovering Who Is In the Community

This basic step of discovering what people, and which public and private organizations, associations and institutions are present in the community is an important step. Seasoned Women want to know everything the community holds in terms of people power and resources. Its Soulful Citizens.

Organizations and Associations

Seasoned Women want to involve and include as many representatives and Soulful Citizens as possible from:
• Artistic organizations (e.g., musical, theatrical, writing, painting),
• Business organizations (e.g., Chamber of Commerce, neighborhood business associations, trade groups),
• Charitable groups and drives (e.g., Red Cross, Cancer Society, United Way),
• Church groups (e.g., service, prayer, maintenance, stewardship, acolytes, men's, women's, youth, and senior groups),
• Civic Events (e.g., July 4th, art fairs, Halloween).
• Collectors Groups (e.g., stamps, flowers, antiques)
• Community Support Groups (e.g., "friends" of the library, nursing home auxiliary)
• Elder groups (e.g., Senior Citizens)
• Ethnic Associations (e.g., Sons of Norway, Black Heritage Club, Caballeros de San Juan)
• Health and Fitness Groups (e.g., jogging, exercise, dieting)
• Interest Clubs (e.g., recycling, antique car owners, book groups)
• Local Media (e.g., community radio, TV, newspaper, cable TV)
• Men's Groups (e.g., cultural, political, social, educational, vocational)

• Mutual Support/Self-Help Groups (e.g., AA, Sweat Equity housing programs, La Leche League)
• Neighborhood (e.g., crime watch, block clubs, neighborhood organizations)
• Outdoor Groups (e.g., garden clubs, Audubon society, conservation clubs)
• Political Organizations (e.g., Democrats, Republicans, caucuses)
• School groups (e.g., printing club, PTA, child care)
• Service Clubs (e.g., Zonta, Kiwanis, Rotary, American Association of University Women, fraternities, sororities)
• Social Cause Groups (e.g., peace, rights, advocacy, service)
• Sports Leagues (e.g., bowling, basketball, baseball, fishing, volleyball)
• Study Groups (e.g., literary clubs, bible-study groups)
• Veteran Groups (e.g., American Legion, Amvets, Veterans of Foreign Wars, their auxiliaries)
• Women's Groups (e.g., cultural, political, social, educational, vocational)
• Youth Groups (e.g., Future Farmers, Scouts, YMCA, and YWCA)

Kretzmann and McKnight[18]

It is also necessary to compile a list of the following organizations, groups and associations who are a rich resource in every community for building partnerships:
• Local businesses,
• Churches,
• Nongovernmental agencies,
• City, county, public and governmental institutions,
• Health and human service agencies.

Ask people you know to provide the names of these organizations, groups, and associations that are in the community. Other ways to find out this information:

1. Local Libraries. Librarians are absolutely, hands-down, unbelievably amazing when it comes to finding/knowing information. They know who is in the community. Plus, many libraries have directories such as the *Encyclopedia of Associations* and *Self-Help Directories* which are a source for discovering who/what is in the community.
2. Looking through local newspapers and magazines for mention of organizations, groups and associations.
3. Leafing through the local white and yellow pages of the phone book.
4. The local hospital can usually provide information on community organizations, groups, and associations.
5. Asking the Library, the Parks and Recreational Department, and churches which groups use their meeting rooms.

Individual Sources of People Power

There are some Community-Building Models that focus on a community's needs, problems, and deficiencies. These models sometimes view some groups of people as being liabilities, rather than assets, particularly those who lives may depend upon social-service systems or institutions.

The model suggested for Seasoned Women and Soulful Citizen Activists instead focuses on building community based on its strengths, assets, and people power. Seasoned Women know that EVERYONE has gifts, talents, and skills! Seasoned women know that strong communities are those that identify, value, and utilize the capacities of everyone possible and seek to involve and include everyone, even those who have been pushed to the margins of society or who may not be viewed as assets. According to Kretzmann and McKnight (1993) these people may include:

• **People with Disabilities**. The disabled have the same needs as anyone for dignity, friendship, pleasure, and for being part of a community and contributing their gifts, talents, and skills. They allow us to activate our highest, best and most compassionate natures in a relationship that is an enriching privilege and a source of inspiration.
• **Low Income People**. Every person who has low income or needs welfare assistance possesses skills, abilities, and experiences that the community can draw upon. Being labeled and stigmatized only serves to isolate and marginalize them painfully and the community ends up losing their much-needed talents and energies.
• **Young People**. Brimming with happy energy, creativity, ideas, dreams, desires, enthusiasm, and time, youth are no longer viewed as liabilities but rather as an essential foundational piece to building strong communities. Projects that connect youth with other youth and with adults bring a crucial vitality to the community.
• **The Elders**. Throughout history, a society's elders have been recognized as the carriers of experience, knowledge, and wisdom accumulated over a lifetime. But with our industrialized societies, they have become invisible, marginalized and stripped of their dignity and their contribution. Labeled as the Elderly and as Seniors, they have come to be viewed by some as useless drains on the economy, the medical and social services. Seasoned women do not perpetuate these myths that rob their communities of a vast reservoir of economic resources, culture, tradition, a sense of

history, experience, knowledge, skills, talents, and time.

• **People with Artistic Gifts**. The purpose of artists, writers, dancers, actors, musicians, etc. is not just for our entertainment. The role of the artist is very serious and crucial. They help us navigate through fear, chaos, and heartbreak in changing times. They help us to understand what is happening around us and within us. They comfort our hearts and nourish our souls. They pull us through. They show us our outmoded thinking and how to transcend it. They inspire us to play and imagine and open ourselves to the field of all possibilities, to dream ourselves into an authentic life of purpose and meaning.

Kretzmann and McKnight[19]

Seasoned Women need to know who is in the community, the individuals, the public institutions, the private sector, the associations, and organizations; the spaces and facilities, materials and equipment; the economic resources. Seasoned Women want to know the assets of the community. Based on Kretzmann and McKnight (1993) the following is a sample of the kinds of information that can be gathered, in a check-list form, from individual people in terms of their skills, gifts, knowledge, resources, and wisdom.

I. Skills Information
Health
__ Caring for the Elderly
__ Caring for the Mentally Ill
__ Caring for the Sick
__ Caring for the Physically Disabled or Developmentally Disabled

If the above items are answered yes, discover the kind of care provided by asking:

Never Doubt

__ Bathing
__ Feeding
__ Preparing Special Diets
__ Exercising and Escorting
__ Grooming
__ Dressing
__ Making the person feel at ease

Office

__ Keyboard (words per minute _____)
__ Operating Adding Machine/Calculator
__ Filing Alphabetically/Numerically
__ Taking Phone Messages
__ Writing Business Letters (not typing)
__ Receiving Phone Orders
__ Operating a Switchboard
__ Keeping Track of Supplies
__ Bookkeeping
__ Entering Information into Computer
__ Word Processing

Construction and Repair

__ Painting
__ Porch Construction or Repair
__ Tearing Down Buildings
__ Knocking Out Walls
__ Wall papering
__ Furniture Repairs
__ Repairing Locks
__ Building Garages
__ Bathroom Modernization
__ Building Room Additions
__ Tile Work
__ Installing Drywall & Taping
__ Plumbing Repairs
__ Electrical Repairs
__ Bricklaying & Masonry

__ Cabinet Making
__ Kitchen Modernization
__ Furniture Making
__ Installing Insulation
__ Plastering
__ Soldering & Welding
__ Concrete Work (sidewalks)
__ Installing Floor Coverings
__ Repairing Chimneys
__ Heating/Cooling System Installation
__ Putting on Siding
__ Tuck-pointing
__ Cleaning Chimneys (chimney sweep)
__ Installing Windows
__ Building Swimming Pools
__ Carpentry Skills
__ Roofing Repair or Installation

Maintenance
__ Window Washing
__ Floor Waxing or Mopping
__ Washing and Cleaning Carpets/Rugs
__ Routing Clogged Drains
__ Using a Hand-truck in a Business
__ Caulking
__ General Household Cleaning
__ Fixing Leaky Faucets
__ Mowing Lawns
__ Planning & Caring for Gardens
__ Pruning Trees & Shrubbery
__ Cleaning/Maintaining Swimming Pools
__ Floor Sanding or Stripping
__ Wood Stripping/Refinishing

Food
__ Catering to Large Numbers of People (more than 10)
__ Serving Food to Large Numbers of People

Never Doubt

__ Preparing Meals for Large Numbers of People
__ Clearing/Setting Tables for Large Numbers of People
__ Washing Dishes for Large Numbers of People
__ Operating Commercial Food Preparation Equipment
__ Bar-tending
__ Meat-cutting
__ Baking

Child Care

__ Caring for Babies (under 1-year-old)
__ Caring for Children (1-6)
__ Caring for Children (7-13)
__ Taking Children on Field Trips

Transportation

__ Driving a Car
__ Driving a Van
__ Driving a Bus
__ Driving a Taxi
__ Driving a Tractor Trailer
__ Driving a Commercial Truck
__ Driving a Vehicle/Delivering Goods
__ Hauling
__ Operating Farm Equipment
__ Driving an Ambulance

Operating Equipment & Repairing Machinery

__ Repairing Radios, TVs, VCRs
__ Repairing Other Small Appliances
__ Repairing Automobiles
__ Repairing Trucks/Buses
__ Repairing Auto/Truck/Bus Bodies
__ Using a Forklift
__ Repairing Large Household Equipment
             (e.g., refrigerator)
__ Repairing Heating & Air Conditioning System
__ Operating a Dump Truck

__ Fixing Washers/Dryers
__ Repairing Elevators
__ Operating a Crane
__ Assembling Items

Supervision
__ Writing Reports
__ Filling Out Forms
__ Planning Work for Other People
__ Directing the Work of Other People
__ Making a Budget
__ Keeping Records of All Your Activities
__ Interviewing People

Sales
__ Operating a Cash Register
__ Selling Products Wholesale or for Manufacturer (if so, which products?)
__ Selling Products Retail (if so, which products?)
__ Selling Services (if so, which services?)
How have you sold these products or services?
       __ Door to Door
       __ Phone
       __ Mail
       __ Store
       __ Home

Music
__ Singing
__ Play an instrument (if so, which instrument?)

Security
__ Guarding Residential Property
__ Guarding Commercial Property
__ Guarding Industrial Property
__ Armed Guard
__ Crowd Control

Never Doubt

__ Ushering at Major Events
__ Installing Alarms or Security Systems
__ Repairing Alarms or Security Systems
__ Firefighting

Other

__ Upholstering
__ Sewing
__ Dressmaking
__ Crocheting
__ Knitting
__ Tailoring
__ Moving Furniture or Equipment to Different Locations
__ Managing Property
__ Assisting in the Classroom
__ Hair Dressing
__ Hair Cutting
__ Phone Surveys
__ Jewelry or Watch Repair

II. Community Skills
Have you ever organized or participated in any of the following community activities. Check for yes.

__ Boys Scouts/Girl Scouts
__ Fundraisers
__ Bingo
__ School-Parent Association
__ Sports Teams
__ Camp Trips for Kids
__ Field Trips
__ Political Campaigns
__ Block Clubs
__ Community Groups
__ Rummage Sales
__ Yard Sales
__ Church Suppers

__ Community Gardens
__ Neighborhood Associations
__ Other Groups or Community Work

Kretzmann and McKnight[20]

Part Two: Building relationships

Creating a successful and sustainable community is not about Seasoned Women finding some sort of structure to impose on a community. There is no hard-and-fast blueprint. No one-size-fits-all. Creating community is a process. A living process. A living system. To unfold. To let emerge.

Living systems are
•Intelligent, learning constantly,
•Creative, finding new ways to express themselves,
•Adaptive, changing when necessary, always exploring new possibilities,
•Self-organizing.

Seasoned Women do not need to contrive ways to force these characteristics onto communities; they only need to find ways to evoke them. They just need to set the community free.

A community's strength comes from the many and varied links it can form within and across all the different sectors that comprise a community. As relationships between community members and organizations grow, so do their energy, excitement, and confidence in meeting the challenges it faces. Members gain trust in their own creativity and ingenuity. People begin to look less and less to the outside for help and more and more to each other.

In the county where I initiated the America's Promise vision for providing children with a solid foundation, by the end of three years, I had managed to build partnerships with—and between—over 100 community businesses, nonprofit organizations, schools, social agencies, local government and faith communities. They formulated specific written statements of commitment towards the goals and we then shared them with everyone else in the community.

A few examples include:

Asbury United Methodist Church promises to expand their Wednesday afternoon safe place to 5:30 p.m., eventually offering structured after-school activities five afternoons a week, including a meal. Also pledges to offer volunteer tutoring opportunities to high-school students. Will explore the possibility of developing a mentoring program.

Citrus and Chemical Bank will allow employees paid time-off to volunteer in the community. We will make voluntary, concrete commitments of goods, services, volunteers, or funding to the America's Promise goals.

City Police Department promises to assist in development of a youth volunteer program. Commits to offering a community room for meetings. Promises to develop 2-3 Neighborhood Service Centers as Safe Places, using volunteers to offer structured activities and homework help.

Explorations Children's Museum pledges to offer five staff members to work with area agencies or schools to mentor children. Commits to offer our building and to share resources for community projects or meetings and to assist other agencies in providing programs.

Merrill Lynch promises to involve all employees in reading program at two elementary school and two middle schools by the fall. Will make financial contributions to area schools.

The Electric Company promises to encourage employee volunteerism through a point system and recognition and allow paid time-off to volunteer. Opportunities will be posted on bulletin boards and other routes of communication. We pledge to become a Work-to-School with the County School System offering shadowing and mentoring opportunities to students. We will support increasing numbers of students in the "About Face" program. We pledge to evaluate needs and requests for concrete commitments of goods, services, volunteers or funding, expanding services as necessary.

Department of Labor and Security Employment, Division of Jobs and Benefits, promises to help youth 16 and older who have physical, mental, and emotional disabilities to obtain or maintain employment.

Imperial Symphony Orchestra promises to work with Holland and Knight Law Firm to match three musically gifted students from disadvantaged homes with Symphony musicians for instruction in classical music and other related opportunities.

Holland and Knight promises to match employees with students from the J.K. Elementary School for tutoring and one-on-one instruction. Promises to sponsor family dinners to give families a special evening out, enabling teachers to meet and speak to parents. Will participate in "Take Your Child to Work Day" giving students books, educational materials, gifts, tours, and reading to them. Volunteers will meet with students for special cultural activities outside school. Will award all tutoring students family memberships to the Children's Museum. Will work with Imperial Symphony Orchestra to match three musically-gifted students from disadvantaged homes with Symphony musicians for instruction in classical music and other related opportunities.

Department of Children and Families promises to encourage employee volunteerism through the "I Care" committee. Pledges to allow employees time-off to volunteer in charitable community projects.

Floral Elementary School promises to add 10 more high-school volunteers to tutor and mentor students. Pledges to expand our holiday service projects for an additional 20 families.

Habitat for Humanity promises to offer training and volunteer opportunities to six entry-level construction workers (16 and older) who will commit to 80 hours of on-the-job training. Pledges to offer volunteer administrative opportunities to three additional high-school students. Commits to increase the number of youth volunteer opportunities on Saturday to 40 hours a month.

M.A.D. D.A.D.S. promises to increase the number of students in our tutoring and mentoring program. Will offer an after-school program, to meet every day for youth ages K-9. Will recruit resource personnel to speak at local high schools on health issues, drug awareness, and dealing with peer pressure.

Part Three: Mobilizing

Seasoned Women want to know who is in the community not only to determine the community's assets but because it is important to invite as many people from the various sectors as possible to participate, NOT only because of their particular skills, gifts, talents, and experiences, but because they are part of the community. They are stakeholders in the overall social and economic health and well-being of the community. They are needed to commit to the mission and vision of the community.

Communities that nurture relationships between the people coming from different sectors begin to appreciate each others' capabilities, skills, talents, gifts, and resources, rather than dwelling on the community's deficits. The communities that are more successful are the ones who have defined their identity based on setting free the capacities of its members within the context of their own unique history, architecture, culture, and natural surroundings.

In a thorough examination of the community-building process, Mattessich and Monsey (1997) of Wilder Research Center identified what factors of the process lead to success.

Widespread participation tops the list as a major contribution to the strength of the community. The more people involved from various sectors that align with the mission and vision not only provides a diverse pool of a community's resources, but it is crucial to the accomplishing of tasks, meeting challenges, and making decisions.

Additionally, when the community is involved in a collective effort, there is an increased possibility that there will be a political acceptance of activities, programs and policies. And that is as it should be: People dictating their own politics, programs and policies, not politics dictating policies and programs to the people.[21]

Other characteristics of successful community-building include:
• **Good System of Communication.** Seasoned Women need to develop a system of communication, not only within the community, but outside the community as well, with the rest of the world. Good communication

serves to keep residents aware, which in turn helps maintain the motivation to participate. Ongoing communication provides information about plans, initiatives and what is being accomplished. By allowing citizens to see results and to know that their efforts in the community are effective and needed, the impetus is created that they need to continue their contribution and involvement. Good systems of communication enable citizens to assemble and act quickly in the face of sudden obstacles or crises.

Good methods of communicating can use a variety of techniques that range from newsletters, news releases, public meetings, social media, neighborhood information brokers and networks to special events such as festivals, parties, and parades.

• **Minimal Competition Between Community Organizations.** Seasoned Women can realize greater success when the different sectors do not feel that they are competing with each other for resources or leadership. Success calls for as many people as possible to align themselves with the mission and the vision, and for there to be a spirit of collaboration allowing each member or organization to contribute what it is they do best and eliminating the duplication of activities.

• **Benefits Many Residents.** The success of a community-building initiative is directly proportionate to the number of citizens it benefits and how visible those benefits are.

• **Focus Simultaneously on Both the Process and the Results.** Seasoned Women will find that building relationships (which is a process) is every bit as important a component of community building as achieving the goals (that is, the results). Relationships between community members, and the spirit of valuing relationship and collaboration, become an enduring and embedded cultural identity and practice that spills over into other aspects of community life and living together.

• **Thorough Gathering of Information.** Successful efforts depend on the crucial first step of spending the necessary time and resources towards gaining knowledge about the community and compiling information about all those who comprise the community. It is the crucial first step that informs the decision about what the second step is to take. There is the extra-added benefit in this step, in that it begins the community-building process, of involving others, and building relationships.

• **Early Involvement and Support From Established Organizations.** Early on, Seasoned Women should seek the support and involvement of long-standing organizations in the community, be they religious, civic, governmental, or educational groups or agencies. They help to legitimize the community initiative. They already have solid relationships built in the community. They have access to resources, personnel, facilities, knowledge, and equipment.

• **Community Control Over Decision-Making.** Initiatives are more successful when community members participate in reaching decisions. It can happen that agencies and organizations providing resources or funding might also come with their own agendas and requirements. Seasoned Women must become skillful and flexible at managing these outside agendas with the critical need for the initiative to stay autonomous and responsive to the community's efforts and needs and the mission and vision upon which it is founded. The initiative will not survive if it becomes co-opted by outside agencies and agendas. Initiatives can fall apart under requirements placed upon them by funders or other agencies and organizations.[22]

Part Four: Convening the Community and Developing the Vision and a Plan

When it comes to living processes and the act of creating, community building is no different than every other living, creative process. When it comes to the splendid work of creation, there is quite a predictable thing that happens. Things can get messy. They can start to look fuzzy. They may reach a point of feeling so chaotic that one wonders if the whole initiative is impossible to accomplish.

When living processes are in the middle of organizing and creating themselves into more complex and effective systems, they must go through this experience of seeming like it is all going kablooey. It is. It can feel scattered and senseless. It is. But this is an unavoidable happening along the road to success.

If Seasoned Women want creativity to flourish, it is wise to become comfortable with chaos. It's a package deal. Expect it; manage it; and use it to keep moving the initiative into the light of accomplished goals and vision.

Unfortunately most of our institutions currently arrange themselves around fierce attempts to keep things predictable and controllable and establish all kinds of rules and regulations, policies, and rigid role assignments. When creativity moves into its chaotic-looking phase, it can strike fear in many hearts. Consequently, in too many of our organizations, when creativity emerges, and with it some measure of chaos, the chaos can get squelched mighty quickly, and with it, the creativity.

It's not easy to hang tough when there are temporary set-backs or failures, or pressure and resistance from the outside. When different groups come together with their different ideas, it can take on a scattered, unfocused feel. It can seem far easier to retreat to more traditional structures and solutions. The temptation can be to fall back into the perceived safety of our old rigid structures.

Here is what is essential for the Seasoned Woman to remember:

Do not be afraid that the initiative is going to absolutely spin itself off into oblivion.

According to Margaret Wheatley's research into organizational behavior (1994), mathematicians can create computerized models of chaos. As the model takes action, it looks random and haphazard and totally nonsensical. But only for a while. If watched long enough, a beautiful and coherent form emerges and begins to take shape.[23]

It is the same for initiatives and organizations. Out of the chaos, form emerges. This same force that keeps it all together, whether it be in the galaxies of the universe or the smallest of human cells or in a community organization, has been called a "strange attractor." A magnetic force. A gravitational pull. So alive is it in the cauldron of creativity that it begins to draw everything together.

In organizations this strange attractor ultimately manifests as *meaning*. In the midst of turbulence, non-sense, struggles, and tough times, it is those initiatives in which members hold steadfastly to their purpose and meaning, to the mission and the vision, that will see it take shape and succeed.[24]

Leadership

Seasoned Women know their intention for being together. They stay clear and strong on their purpose and the meaning for coming together. They exchange, provide, and create information and data. Information belongs to everyone and it is crucial when organizing quickly and effectively.

Seasoned Women stimulate and facilitate relationships between the different participants. People need access to each other. They need help making connections.

Seasoned Women are alert to changes from any direction. They are willing to change, adapt, and evolve. They embrace the messiness of creativity. They know that chaos and order are two sides of the same coin. They help others to embrace it and recognize it for its inevitability and the important gifts it comes bearing: growth and more creativity.

They learn constantly, developing wisdom as they go. They pay attention to results.

Seasoned Women know that they are NOT the sole provider of the initiative's vision. They are NOT the sole inspiration and source of its ideas. They are NOT the sole person responsible for the initiative's intelligence.

According to The National Commission on Neighborhoods (as cited by Mattessich and Monsey), successful initiatives report that "A local leader, or set of leaders, lit the spark that brought about the initiative ... individuals with a view of a problem, or problems, and ideas of what had to be done in order to begin to solve them."[25]

Successful initiatives do not rely too heavily on the person or persons who ignited the original spark to take action. Instead, they generate new leaders over time in order to replace those who leave, and, to fill new roles. As the effort grows in the community so does the need for people to lead different tasks and fill different roles. Allowing for diversity and different styles greatly enhances the effort and the decision-making process.[26]

Seasoned Women can adopt the five character-istics of community organizers, identified by Mattes-sich and Monsey that lead to a greater chance of suc-cess.

1) Understanding the community, with all its

a. Culture of belief patterns, social norms, traditions of community residents, religious and ethnic orien-tations, which influences daily living and decision-making.

b. Social Structure, existing social networks be-tween residents; knowing which members assume which roles such as task accomplishment or sup-port roles such as morale building.

c. Demographics and the characteristics of the com-munity's population, age groups, ethnicity, living ar-rangements and housing patterns.

d. Political structures and the formal and informal power relationships that exist in the community.

e. Issues of major concerns of the residents.

2) Sincerity of the Commitment, displaying

a. Interest in the community's long-term well-being.

b. Sustained attachment to community members.

c. Honesty.

d. Actions that serve the interests of the whole community.

3) Relationship of Trust, which includes

a. Sharing a common mission and vision.

b. Looking out for the best interests of the commun-ity, not being exploitative.

c. Not favoring one group over another.

d. A common vocabulary and the same understand-ing when communicating.

e. Following through on commitments.

4) Ability to Organize, which includes

a. To realistically appraise requirements for com-pleting work.

b. To work with and motivate people.

c. To plan activities and be productive.

5) Ability to be Flexible and Adaptable

a. To changing situations, people, politics and social climates.

b. To the changing needs of the community.[27]

Successful Communities

Seasoned Women getting involved and leading the way, mobilizing other Soulful Citizen Activists in the building and rebuilding of our local communities, around specific core issues, across the many tracks of civil society, is our last, best hope to create the kind of nation that is healthy and sustainable, one that allows the many, and not just the few, to thrive and flourish.

At this critical juncture on our planet, in our country and across our nation, as we and the rest of the world stagger between survival and extinction, there can be no higher and more urgent calling than for Seasoned Women to bring forth their passion and wisdom. We are an inextricable part and the latest creation of this unfolding 13-billion-year-old awesome mystery of life and love.

We are stewards of a four-billion-year-old planet. We are members of a seven-million-year-old human species living in a nearly 240-year-old nation founded upon the high principles and visions of a people who honor as its highest calling the same principles and vision that guide the universe: connection, cooperation, freedom, creativity, and expansion from the simple to a more complex life.

Communities that reflect and duplicate this very same recipe for success, that share certain social and psychological ingredients are the most successful.

Mattessich and Monsey found that communities that recognize a need for change and who are aware of the issues become charged with inspiration.

When an initiative serves the many, and not just a few, there is an increase in participation. When it grows from within, rather than being imposed from without, when the residents themselves generate the ideas, goals and activities, when the geographic area is small enough to build relationships between residents and manage the activities, where flexibility and adaptability are used in problem-solving and getting things done, success takes hold.

Communities that are successful are those in which members stay open when dealing with issues and use different ways to accomplish tasks, when they can be responsive to changing goals and objectives, when they are able to come together in a spirit of collaboration and cooperation, trust and communication.

And finally, communities that meet with the greatest success are those whose leadership can be strongly identified, who have members who step forward to act as spokespersons and who motivate residents with a clear mission and a strong vision, those who can stir within residents an eager willingness to listen and follow and join in taking action.[28]

While all the parts of a community and civil society sectors exist to serve their own specific missions while they also support the overall social needs of the community with its collective mission, visions, and goals. Seasoned Women, leading and mobilizing other Soulful Citizen Activists are a fierce powerhouse of potential, a mighty resource when needing to provide, "bases by which people can exert influence over the direction of their society and resist other groups or the government when they are seen to impinge unjustly on their interests, activities or purposes."[29]

Never Doubt

"I do not believe that meditation and prayer will change the world. I believe what we need is action."

His Holiness, The 14th Dalai Lama

CHAPTER EIGHT

Blessed Are the Peacemakers

Benjamin Franklin once said there are only two things certain in life: death and taxes.

I would add a third: CONFLICT!

Conflict is inevitable. Wherever there are human beings in relationship to each other, some sort of conflict is going to eventually arise. Wise, foresightful, and Seasoned Women plan for it.

Human beings are in the process of transitioning from a regressive, stunted, and restricted way of being in the world into a more progressive, expansive, and inclusive one. Unfortunately this transformation is not without its painful physical and emotional challenges. Human beings must now face the consequences of their past actions. The chickens have come home to roost and we find ourselves with multiple and converging environmental, political, social, and economic disasters all demanding simultaneously urgent address.

As Seasoned Women, we know that there are people who have been avoiding acknowledging the unprecedented peril we have brought upon ourselves. When untoward external circumstances finally force them awake, they may unleash any number of strong, yet predictable, responses. While these reactions are rooted in fear, along a continuum ranging from apprehensiveness to abject terror, they will show up in people as feelings of overwhelm, denial, resistance, anger, despair, violence, depression, anxiety, anguish, paralysis, suffering, etc.

Add to these reactions the usual and customary conflicts that emerge as groups of people, in relationship to each other, work together to bring changes, and it is the wise Seasoned Woman who prepares for there to be clashes and collisions. It is a wise Seasoned Woman who equips herself with knowledge and tools and fierce courage and compassion to wade into the fray of conflict and upset and anger, in her local, national or international community, determined to enable it to be transformed into positive outcomes.

I believe that our world is on the verge of self-destruction and death because the society as a whole has so deeply neglected that which is most human and most valuable and the most basic of all the works of love: the work of human communication, of caring and nurturance, of tending the personal bonds of community.

Beverly Wildung Harrison

Concepts

Our culture has developed very few positive ways of how to go about working out our differences. Consequently, our usual default methods have become limited to varying degrees of avoidance or violence. For many, when it comes to high levels of dread and loathing, dealing with conflict ranks right up there with birthdays, public speaking and going to the dentist.

In the years following WWII, the field of Conflict Resolution saw an increase in its growth and development with the realization that neither governments nor economic systems are capable of bringing peace, balance, cooperation and collaboration. Pulling from across the many disciplines of Sociology, Psychology, Economics, Religion, International Relations, Anthropology, Mathematics, and Philosophy, there sprung up a wide body of interdisciplinary quantitative and qualitative research and analyses around the nature, causes and processes of conflict as it relates to war, traditional diplomacy, class struggles, organizational conflict, labor disputes, revolutions, game theory, the nature of relationships that spanned the gamut, from interpersonal and community to national and international relationships.

Today the field of Conflict Resolution has become an established academic discipline, a field of study, both an art and a science, offering both undergraduate and graduate degrees, vast and diverse in its knowledge of examining the relationship between human beings and each other when it comes to power and conflict. There exists a broad array of tools, techniques and practices for intermediaries, intervenetions, de-escalation, nonviolent solutions, problem-solving, peacebuilding, peacekeeping, and conflict prevention.[30]

When it comes to mediation, the history and practice can be traced back as far as Greek and Roman times.[31] While it is true that humans have too often used violence as a way to deal with their quarrels, history also teaches us that humans have long employed nonviolent ways to solve their disputes. Mediation and alternative ways of dealing with conflict are noted throughout many of the world's major religious sects of Judaism, Islam, Christianity, Hinduism, Buddhism, Confucianism, as well as among the Puritans and Quakers, and indigenous cultures the world over, led by their elders and shamans.[32]

All around the world, from the Polynesian to the Kpelle people of Liberia to the Abkhazian people in the Caucasus Mountains of Georgia to the Yoruba in

Nigeria, people use talking and mediation to settle their disputes. The Bushmen of Kalahari are a traditional hunting-gathering tribe living on the arid plains of Namibia and Botswana. Like most of the rest of us, they find themselves getting into their fair human share of scraps and scrapes with each other over the usual things like mates, food, and land. But instead of warring it out amongst and between themselves, they bring people together to listen to both sides. If the dispute gets a little scary and intense, certain tribe members are appointed to go and hide all the poisoned arrows, much like implementing gun-control measures. If the altercation involves a larger group, all members, both men and women, are brought together to talk, and talk, and talk it out. Each and every person is included and everyone gets to have their say. It takes as long as it takes to talk it all out, mediate the dispute and then build consensus.[33]

All around the world, there are literally thousands of different and legitimate ways for parties to reach an agreement. Just because <u>we</u> feel comfortable with one set of rules and etiquette does not mean that it is necessarily the most logical, efficient or desirable method for everyone.
Jan Jung-Min Sunoo

Seasoned and wise women elders know that conflict is inevitable and natural and that disagreements need a safe and open place for expression and resolution. Throughout history and around the world, appointed leaders and wise elders continue to use the time-honored practice of mediation and talking it out to resolve infighting, rows, brawls, scuffles, free-for-alls, skirmishes, tussles, and set-tos.

When conflict and disagreement are *not* managed, it can begin a downward spiral that is marked by a sequence of events. First the problem emerges, with one or more of the parties refusing to acknowledge there is a problem, and/or one or more of the other parties escalating their activities to bring attention to their issue(s). Next, people begin to choose sides. Then people with similar views cluster and talk more amongst themselves, and less with those holding dissimilar views. The result is that positions harden and rigidity sets in as it regards how they define both the problem and their "opponents." Information can become distorted and exchanged hit-or-miss. Communication starts to become edgy; misunderstandings more frequent; objectivity declines; perceptions about the character and motives of others begins to twist. There is a tendency to begin looking outside the community for help or for support. The community or the project has hit a crisis point.

What happens next can vary, and can include litigation, lawyers, judges, increasing costs, government agencies, outside regulators, imposed regulations, violence, vandalism, vindictiveness, personal injury, damaged reputations, fractured relationships, community upheaval and a lost opportunity for managing the dispute among themselves.[34]

Guiding Principles

When it comes to assisting a community in problem-solving their conflicts, there are ten guiding principles worth keeping in mind:

Principle #1. Conflicts are a mix of procedures, relationships and substance.
Principle #2. To find a good solution, you have to understand the problem.
Principle #3. Take time to plan a strategy and follow it through.

Principle #4. Progress demands positive working relationships.

Principle #5. Negotiation begins with a constructive definition of the problem.

Principle #6. Parties should help design the process and the solution.

Principle #7. Lasting solutions are based on interests, not positions.

Principle #8. The process must be flexible.

Principle #9. Think through what might go wrong.

Principle #10. Do no harm.[35]

Our first task in approaching another people, another culture, another religion, is to take off our shoes, for the place we are approaching is holy. Else we may find ourselves treading on someone's dreams; more serious still, we may forget that God was there before our arrival.

Max Warren

This chapter provides an overview—an outline—of a generalized, citizen-friendly, community conflict management model for resolving public disputes. It is based on the work of Susan L. Carpenter and W. J. D. Kennedy in *Managing Public Disputes: A Practical Guide for Government, Business, and Citizens' Groups,* a step-by-step process for how to analyze the conflict, design a strategy, adopt procedures, bring those in conflict together, develop options, reach agreements and carry them out.

Please note that that each step and each topic warrants delving into further for a deepening of information and guidance. Keep in mind also that many communities have at their disposal local organizations whose professional expertise lies in mediation and dispute resolution. They are an invaluable resource to contact for advice, suggestions, and involvement when a Seasoned Woman endeavors to intervene in community troubles to find enduring solutions to community conflict.

Basic Steps in a Community Conflict Resolution Process:

I. Prepare a Plan
A. Analyse the Conflict

First of all, are the parties involved interested in a community conflict resolution process? For the process to work, all the parties need to support the effort.

If they do want it, begin to collect information about the dispute through: *Direct observation* of how the parties conduct themselves and how they talk about the issues.

Secondary sources can provide information about how the events unfolded leading up to the conflict as well as what were the prior relationships between the parties. These sources can include newspaper and magazine articles, reports, events, and minutes of meetings.

Personal interviews, which provides the best source of information about the situation, a wider scope of perspectives and a peek into the subtleties of issues.

General categories of questions can include:
"What is your view of the situation?
"What issues are important to you (your group)?
"What other individuals or groups are involved?
"Who else should I be talking to (on all sides)?
"How do you think this problem can be solved?"[36]

After interviewing each party it is useful to organize their input into a chart using the headings:
• Parties
• Issues
• Interests

- Importance of Issues (high, medium, low)
- Sources of power/influence
- Positions/options
- Interest in working with other parties
- Other comments

After organizing and charting this input from the parties, look at the information and begin to look for areas of common interest, conflicting views, where issues cluster and how agreements might be put together. Remembering that conflict is dynamic and thereby leaving room for change and flexibility, this lays the foundation for how to move onto the next step in the process.

B. Designing a Strategy

Every conflict is different and there is no single resolution template that fits every conflict. However, when it comes to designing a strategy there are certain tasks that remain constant and need to be accomplished:

1. Define the problem. Being as concise as possible will enable the best development of an optimal strategy.

2. Identify external constraints. For example, are there parties who are working under deadlines? Legal proceedings? Have the time to participate?

3. Establish a conflict management goal. Goals can include the exchange of information with the parties; identifying interests and issues; inviting parties to develop options that will satisfy their interests; developing joint recommendations; ways to reach agreement.

4. Selecting a meeting structure. Based on the conflict management goals, the meeting structure should support those goals. There are four different types of structures: public meetings; Task groups and advisory

committees; Problem-solving workshops; Formal negotiation sessions.

5. Identifying process steps.

a. Adopt procedures. Parties should always understand the process being proposed.

b. Educate the parties. Determine how much the parties need to be educated on the problem, the issues, and the parties' interests.

c. Generate options. If options exist, begin combining them into proposals. If options have not yet been developed, or the position of parties has become entrenched, more time will be needed to generate options that are acceptable to the parties.

d. Reach agreements. Together, parties decide how to establish criteria by which to consider options, construct agreements, check with their constituents, and agree on the final proposal.

Determining who should participate. Answer these four questions:

1. "What form of participation makes sense?"[37] Decide between involving just representatives or if it should be open to anyone who is interested.

2. "What general categories of participants should be present?"[38] Decide which interests need to be clustered into categories and who/how best to represent them either by individuals or by an overall organization or group.

3. "How many participants should represent each category?"[39] When agreements are reached through consensus, it is not necessary to have equal numbers of representatives from each category. One person from one category can block an agreement. A good size for a working group is 10-12 people. Larger groups are beneficial for bringing a wider base of knowledge and opinions and/or when the issues are more complex and/or there are many parties involved. Larger groups require

more time for reaching agreements. Thirty people can negotiate successfully.

4. "What specific individuals can best represent each category?"[40] Involve the parties in deciding this. They can either select representatives from their own organizations or they can be asked to comment on an overall list of proposed participants.

Defining other roles. In addition to participants, there are other roles that may need to be identified and filled during the negotiation process. They can include:

1. Initiator. The person who suggests there is a dispute that needs resolving.

2. Convener. The person who brings the parties together.

3. Sponsor. Those who encourage parties to come together.

4. Chairperson. The person who opens and closes meetings; helps the group follow the agenda; sees that the process runs smoothly.

5. Facilitator. The person who manages the discussion to see that the group focuses on issues and reaches their goals, establishes the agenda, enforces ground rules, keeps the discussion on track.

6. Recorder. This person summarizes the points of discussion, the decisions made; these are displayed on a wall or a board, so all can see.

7. Technical resource expert. Usually they are not formal participants but are present to answer any technical or legal questions.

8. Logistical support person. This person schedules meetings, makes the arrangements, and compiles and sends out notices to the participants.

9. Observers. These people may have a special interest or knowledge about the conflict. They may be important to carrying out agreements that are made.

10. Mediator. If needed, a third party called in to analyze the conflict, design a strategy or manage the process.

Considering other process issues. Timing, location, funding needs and news media involvement. Everyone involved needs to have an idea of how long the process will take; where meetings will be held; how much it will cost to support the process; and decide whether the process is open to the news media.

C. Set Up a Program
1. Prepare a written description of the process to give to those who are interested or involved.
2. Secure funding, if needed.
3. Develop ground rules. These are the rules of conduct for those participating in the process. They should be shared ahead of time so that parties can contribute to crafting them and agree to abide by them.
4. Invite participants. Invite orally, confirm in writing, restating the purpose of coming together and their role.
5. Confirm roles. Provide participants with a detailed explanation of what is being asked of them to do.
6. Notify interested groups. Those who are interested but are not being invited to participate might like to receive information defining the problem, goals, process and a list of participants.
7. Deal with the news media. Prepare a press kit that includes a description of the problem, goals, overview of the process, who will be involved in the discussion and the name of a person who can be contacted for additional information.
8. Assemble background material. Participants will be provided packets that include background of problem, issues that relate to it, reports, historical documents,

newspaper clippings, and anything else that might be relevant. Also include a list of participants by name, title, affiliations and contact information.

9. Arrange the first meeting. First meetings usually include introductions, procedures, a proposal of the process, ground rules, a history of the problem. Only after there is an agreement about these details should there commence a discussion about issues.

II. Conducting a Program

A. Adopt Procedures. Participants should give their approval of a statement of the problem; the goals; the steps of the process; a method for reaching decisions; the amount of time expected to complete the process; a set of ground rules, how those ground rules will be applied and enforced; how to change rules if needed.

B. Educate Parties. Each participant is asked to describe to other participants their perception of the problem, the issues, their concerns and interests. This collective list becomes the basis for developing options.

C. Develop Options. Create a broad variety of many proposals for possible solutions. At this stage do not critique the proposals or spend time assessing their viability, just create a collection of ideas for solutions.

D. Reach Agreements. While reaching agreements can be achieved in a variety of ways there is a basic sequence of steps to follow:

1. Establish objective criteria. Working together, establish guidelines for determining the acceptance or appropriateness of a proposal based on the list of interests and any other factors that must be considered for the viability of an agreement.

2. Apply criteria to existing options. Evaluate proposals based on the agreed-upon criteria.

3. Reach consensus on options.

4. Produce a draft agreement.

5. Present the draft for review and agreement.

6. Reach final agreement.

III. Carrying Out Agreements

A. Establish a Monitoring System. Parties must agree on a way to ensure that agreements are honored. This can be done by appointing a public official or agency or a committee made up of participants who were involved in the process. It serves as a central place if parties have concerns or suggestions.

B. Work Out Details. With regard to agreements, participants need to specify steps to be taken, identifying those who will accomplish them and a time frame for completion.

C. Renegotiate Sections. Sometimes it becomes necessary to renegotiate an agreement, for example, if new information surfaces. The parties need to develop an agreement on a process they can follow.

D. Handle Violations. It is the monitoring committee who will explore the nature of the violation of the agreement. If the reason is deemed legitimate then there must be alternative methods developed for solving the problem. But if a party is just being irresponsible, the committee must act decisively to either enforce any agreed-upon consequences for breaching the agreement, or bring peer pressure to bear from the other parties or from the public at large to enlist the party to honor the agreement. This is only fair to all the parties and it is necessary so that the agreement can fulfilled.[41]

Dialogue vs. Debate

Sometimes what starts as a discussion ends up as a debate. There is a big difference between dialogue and debate. Dialogue can be defined as "the coming together of persons who desire to learn and grow in the truth through building on the insights and observations of another, particularly an adversary."[42]

Blessed Are the Peacemakers

Dialogue seeks to include everyone and increase their understanding of themselves and others, while debate is the arguing of one's position in hopes of overcoming a perceived opponent. A goal of dialogue is to identify and build a group's inner strength while debate searches for weaknesses in order to discount and devalue another. In dialogue questions are asked to clarify one's understanding of what is being said while in debate asking questions is a tactic used to confuse and trip up others. In dialogue, words and feelings are honored. In debate they are used to criticize, distort and invalidate others.[43]

Ground Rules for Useful Discussions

Think together about what you want to get out of your discussions.

Listen carefully to others in order to really understand what they are saying, especially when their ideas differ from your own.

When disagreement occurs, keep talking. Stay curious, rather than judgmental. Explore the disagreement. Search for common concerns beneath the surface.

Try to avoid building your own arguments in your head while others are talking.

Help to develop one another's ideas. Listen carefully and ask clarifying questions.

Be open to changing your mind; ideally about the issue at hand, but minimally about the person(s) holding the opposing view.

Value one another's experiences and think about how they have contributed to each person's thinking.

Anecdotal stories have value because they describe our experience and can help us understand what others have gone through. But be careful not to over-generalize from a story.

Speak your mind freely but give others equal time.

Above all, be civil.[44]

The plain fact is that the planet does not need more successful people. But it does desperately need more peacemakers, healers, restorers, story-tellers, and lovers of every kind. It needs people who live well in their places. It needs people of moral courage willing to join the fight to make the world habitable and humane. And these qualities have little to do with success as our culture has defined it.

David Orr, Earth in Mind

CHAPTER NINE

Notes to Self

As the saying goes, "the road to hell is paved with good intentions." And as the rapper Ice Cube's song goes, "so come on and chickity-check yo' self before you wreck yo' self." According to the online Urban Dictionary the definition of "check yo' self" is:

> To check yourself over; to watch yourself before you get your ass whipped.[45]

This is especially good advice for Seasoned Women who are waking up to realize that something has gone terribly wrong, that something is broken, that our planet and our human family are struggling and suffering, that our world is in deep trouble socially, politically, economically and environmentally.

For those determined to by god do something about it, before rushing out the door, it doesn't hurt to mention a few things to keep in mind:

☑ **Notes to Self**

☑ **Item #1**

One does not become enlightened by imagining figures of light, but by making the darkness conscious.

C.G. Jung

There's a curious thing that happens when one endeavors to take public action in the outer world. Soon enough it will begin to reveal the private landscapes of our own inner world. If one is still hoarding unfinished business in the back of the closet, there's just something about becoming an activist that tends to fling those closet doors off their hinges and let all your own junk fall out.

Unless one has first taken the time, the energy and the honest, unflinching courage to muck out one's own subconscious swamps, the chances are great that the good work one is trying to do will actually be stunted, at best; and destructive, at worst. Our own challenges and personal issues are often the driving force behind taking action. However, unhealed wounds have a way of getting in the way of our effecting positive and lasting change.

The archetypal story of Dr. Jekyll and Mr. Hyde was written about all of us. It is easy to identify with the very pleasant face we put on for the outside daytime dealings in which we are nice, pleasant, polite, generous and morally aligned with the highest and purest of intentions.

Then there is our contradictory "shadow" side that we try desperately to hide not only from public view, but from our own view as well. The shadow is the part of us that does not match how we want to see ourselves or how we want others to see us.

When it comes to greed, hate, revenge, violence, narcissism, self-serving motives, egoism, prejudice, bias, aggression, passive-aggression, addictions, selfishness, vindictiveness, anger, fears and self-righteousness, we disassociate with our own; we disown them; we deny that they could ever possibly exist inside our do-good selves.

At some point in the evolution of a Seasoned Woman, there should have come many opportunities to coax the content of our shadow selves out of hiding in order to take a good look in the broad light of day, acknowledging, combing through, picking, sorting, deciding what was worth keeping and then pitching the rest.

There have generally been many opportunities in the life of a Seasoned Woman for self-examination: crises, traumas, and mourning the losses of mates, children, jobs, dreams, youth and beauty. By the time one has become a Seasoned Woman there have usually been instances that have caused the life of a woman's soul to be struck down into a kind of death, a collapsing into blackness onto a cold, hard ground that later becomes a rich, fertile soil of reflection, regeneration and a rebirthing of herself into a new and more complex inner life.

Otherwise, unacknowledged, unprocessed, unhealed shadows become like molten rock inside our earth's surface. Gases rise. Pressure builds. An eruption occurs. And the next thing you know there's red hot lava spewing emotional fragments straight up into the air and hot ash covering over the place; mudslides, avalanches, mowing down entire forests and every living thing in its path; triggering tsunamis, flash floods and earthquakes.

When it comes to one's shadow, if you don't own it, you'll project it.

If you haven't processed it, you'll pass it on.

Want to make a real and lasing difference in the world?

Chickity-check yo' self first!

Yesterday I was clever, so I wanted to change the world. Today I am wise, so I want to change myself.

Rumi

☑ Item #2

"We do not know how to look honestly at the wreckage without a sense of surrender; far easier to just keep dancing and hope someone else fixes it all.

"To accept the full consequences of the degradation of the environment, the explosion of incarceration, the creeping militarization, the dismantling of democracy, the commodification of culture, the contempt for the real, the culture of impunity among the powerful and the zero tolerance towards the weak and the young, requires a courage that seems beyond us."[46]

To stand resolute and unwavering in the pursuit of creating change, when we are in the midst of so many converging catastrophes and so much push back from the powers-that-be, requires the strength of an ox and the endurance of a sled dog.

In his book, *The Hope* (2009), Andrew Harvey, religious scholar and modern-day mystic, cautions us, and those with whom we work, to be ever mindful about not falling into five particular sinkholes:

Disbelief. "You can understand the danger intellectually and even emotionally, but to accept it with your

101

whole being demands a leap of courage you cannot force but have to prepare for. This is because human beings are conditioned to respond to immediate difficulties but find it hard to respond to a whole cluster of looming disasters for which we have no precedent."

Denial. "I used to imagine I was not in denial about what was happening; now I catch myself reeling in and out of denial about a hundred times a day, even as I have been writing this book...What I am discovering is that thinking you are not in denial is perhaps the most dangerous form of denial in a crisis like ours. It is only by having the courage to unmask the way denial plays out in your innermost thinking that you can begin to be useful."

Dread. "How could any half-conscious human being *not* feel dread at the enormous suffering that is erupting all over the world? Facing the depth of my dread has threatened me, at times, with hopelessness. What I have found, however, is that acknowledging my dread and treating it not as a weakness to be repressed at all costs, but as an inevitable response to real circumstances, has helped me to start to heal it. Allowing myself to feel it in my body, in the depths of my gut, has helped me to discover that within my body there is what I can only describe as a lake of luminous, spacious peace in which the pain can eventually dissolve."

Disillusionment. "The hardest part of facing your disillusionment is that...we all collude with the system we are in, partly out of necessity but also out of cowardice and a love of comfort. The great majority of us have been seduced by the promises of the corporate propaganda machines of limitless growth and progress."

The Desire to Cease to Be. "We are now living in a world in which all of us are consciously or unconsciously traumatized by what we can't help knowing about the world crisis, and this trauma and the desperation it induces fuel a host of addictive behaviors that are driving us into the arms of destruction... All of us have times when we long not merely for escape or distraction, but for relief from bearing anguish of lucid compassion and engaged conscience."

"...when you decide that you cannot bear to stand by and must do something real, you will inevitably meet the reality of the self-destructiveness that now drives a great deal of action in the world. If you do not accept that facing this ferocity will bring you to your knees in despair and drive you to wish you had never been born, you will never be able to find the authentic hope that *is* born when you offer up this heartbreak...to heal... and so discover that you can bear it without denial and continue to love life."[47]

☑ Item #3

What About Our Men?

Most women I know have men in their lives who play significant roles: husbands, lovers, fathers, grand-fathers, sons, grandsons, uncles, nephews, pastors and bosses.

When there is talk about the global need for women to take action and leadership positions, there is usually a resounding YES! However, at the same time, there come the whispers of fear, "But what about our men?" "What happens to them?" "What happens to our relationship with them?"

Notes to Self

Legitimate questions. Legitimate fear. We care about our men.

This world is now dying for the lack of balance between the feminine and masculine energies. It is in our economic, environmental, political and social best interests for men and women to share power and leadership.

Men are not flawed by nature. Real men, who are healthy, balanced, and whole, are not randomly violent and hostile. Men's destructiveness and violence is the result of a damaged self-image caused by a narrow social definition of what it means to be a man, a definition founded on fear. While men may exhibit more violence and aggression, they are also capable of showing love, compassion and altruism.

Mature masculinity affirms and supports life. We have many ancient and modern images of men as healers, protectors, lovers and partners with women, men and nature.

There are many wonderful things about being a man, but at the same time there some things that need to be challenged. We need to have a conversation about what we have come to know as manhood with its structures and guidelines. What needs challenging is the way we collectively define what it means to be a man.

This is not so much an individual ill but a social ill that needs a social response, a shift in definition of manhood in our culture. Untangle the social myths and fantasies that our culture holds about what it means to be a man and what it means to be a woman.

The task for both men and women is to recognize the difference between a healthy, balanced masculinity and a destructive, imbalanced patriarchy.

Both men *and* women must unlearn our destructive and narrow definitions and relearn what it means to be healthy, whole and balanced men and women. The most powerful resource we have for transforming ourselves is honest conversation between men and men, women and women, and men and women.

Celebrate our innate differences! Value them equally.

At this time women and men are being called to do different things. Increasing the number of women across all sectors of civil society would broaden our public conversations, expand the scope of inquiry, change the way we think and generate more options towards solving local, national and international challenges.

Men must take an active role in creating a cultural and social shift. Men need to learn how to be allies with females. This is a time that men can work alongside the leadership of women to meet the challenges of our present day world, supporting women as they do the work of repairing the world.

We also need to challenge men to examine their individual beliefs about their role in our global problems and to take a stand that men need to join in partnership with women to become part of the solution.

Men are being educated to compete and win out over others. Rather than allowing their innate caring for others and cooperation towards building a better life for all, their education is instead preparing them for conflict and war. Men need to use their knowledge, not to manipulate others for their own gain, but to heal themselves, others, our community and the world.

Men need to work with women on how to raise our boys into men. We need to teach our boys that it's OK to have a full range of feelings, not just anger. It's OK to promote equality, to be healthy, whole, and balanced. The way we are socializing our boys today is based on fear. It is an immature masculinity. It confuses controlling, threatening, and hostile behavior with strength. It uses pushing, shoving, shouting, and aggression as a way to get their way. It seeks to *over*power others rather than *em*power others.

Mature masculinity is focused, disciplined, clear thinking and exercises power thoughtfully. It channels the energy of aggression into the service of some greater good beyond one's own personal gain.

To become a healthy, whole and balanced man does not mean men need to become more like women. It means allowing men to have, and express, their emotions. It means cultivating the ability to listen deeply and to care for and nurture all forms of life. Emotions, intimacy, and good relationships are not gender-specific.

Living as a healthy, whole, and balanced man celebrates the beauty of nature and the physical world and so protects it and guards it.

Real men, whole and balanced, act with courage, decisiveness, wisdom, and passion. They are protective caretakers of their families, and that family includes the collective family of earth, all its creatures and creations.

Becoming a healthy, whole and balanced man is the dynamic basis for a sacred partnership between men and women. When both men and women balance their sacred masculine and feminine energies, we are going to discover REAL fire for the first time!

Seasoned Women need to gather their courage and their inner strength and do what they know in their hearts needs to be done, to bring forth their wisdom and skills, in glorious acts of loving insurrection, to save the very lives of our men, our children, our communities, our planet, ourselves—and to put a stop to this twisted drama, pain, and insanity.

If we care about the men in our lives; if we really want to help them and repair this ailing world, then we need to do our best as Seasoned Women to fully be women, to stand resolute and ride out the challenges or objections that come when women step forward to claim their rightful place in contributing to decisions and solutions. People will react. Let them. If women stand strong, we can be the catalyst for others to embrace the process of their becoming fully themselves.

It is time for men to reclaim the energy of the heart. For most men, that will only happen once they have processed their reaction to the rise of women that is happening on the planet.

Every human being faces a choice at this time: Do you remain aligned with our fear-based, male-dominated society, or, do you consciously make the move to the more compassionate, egalitarian paradigm that is emerging on our planet?

Notes to Self

We all need to realize that our liberation (as woman or as man) is tied to the liberation of our partners in humanity (of men or of women): while confining roles confine everyone at this time in very different ways, they confine all of us. It is in our social, economic, and political best interests to share power and leadership between men and women. It creates a world that is freer and fairer. It frees us to be the healers, protectors, lovers, and partners that we all innately are.

☑ **Item #4**

A few thoughts on Evil:

Man's inhumanity to man is as old as humanity itself. Some people just do evil things.

Kurt Sutter

There is no explanation for evil. It must be looked upon as a necessary part of the order of the universe. To ignore it is childish, to bewail it is senseless.

W. Somerset Maugham

Sadly, of course, there is real evil in the world. You watch the news and see all the people suffering and so much cruelty.

Angelina Jolie

Evil has its origin in this deeply unconscious predator-prey pattern of behavior...Evil may be defined as the act of inflicting terror, suffering, humiliation, torture or death on an individual or group of individuals, ranging in kind from the murder of a child to the atrocities taking place in Syria to the viciously cruel attacks on others on Facebook or Twitter.

One of the most difficult things to recognize is that each one of us is capable of acting in a hateful, cruel or evil way, or of being complicit in these ways of behaving, whether as an individual or as the member of a government, institution, corporate body or nation.

Anne Baring[48]

I do not want to portray that there is no such thing as manifest and irredeemable evil, for that exists. Throughout time there is the mystical sense that any individuation work done by humans also changes the darkness in the collective unconscious of all humans, that being the place where the predator resides...

I do not claim to know how it all works, but following Archetypal Pattern, it would look something like this:

Instead of reviling the predator, or running away from it, we dismember it.

We accomplish this by not having divisive thoughts...

We dismantle the predator by countering the diatribes with our own nurturant truths...by maintaining our intuitions and instincts and by resisting the predator's seductions.

Clarissa Pinkola Estes[49]

It is time for the Sacred Activist to stop being naïve about the power of the destructive forces both within themselves and in the world...about their own shadows, about the shadow sides of the political, religions, economic and religious establishments or... the occult destructive forces...that wreak havoc if we do not acknowledge their strength and make every wise effort to protect ourselves against them, inwardly and outwardly...

Notes to Self

... in doing sacred work your greatest protections are continual and radical humility, ever more astute discrimination, and a canny prudence. Otherwise, for all your noble intentions and compassionate motivations, your work will be wrecked on the rocks of reality.

Andrew Harvey[50]

☑ **Item #5**

But it turns out that people who are grounded and secure don't change much under stress. That's what being grounded means.

Michael Gruber

Being part of something greater than ourselves, contributing, participating, breathing something good into being that was not there before, something that eases the struggle or empowers the life of another, is the epitome of a soul-satisfying experience.

And there are times that it can also be an unbelievably arduous, exhausting, maddening, gut-wrenching, spirit-sapping, hand-wringing, hair-pulling undertaking.

Activism can be demanding physically and psychologically. It can deplete one of energy and drive and the endurance necessary to push on towards the goal. It is easy to feel overwhelmed with the enormity of the task of changing institutions, attitudes and policies; to witness the suffering of others; and to manage one's righteous anger and indignation over unfair and unjust conditions or practices. It is crucial that Seasoned Women and Soulful Citizen Activists take deliberate good care of themselves to avoid burning out and giving up.

Being vigilant about committing to daily practices that include both spiritual disciplines and physical activity is essential to staying the course of an activist. Rest, renew, focus, stay strong, clear, inspired and keep the internal balance through various combinations that sustain the spiritual and physical stamina:

Aerobics, Zumba, martial arts, weight training, kickboxing, walking, running, hiking, cycling, ice skating, playing a sport, swimming, diving...

Yoga, Tai Chi, Qigong, Pilates, an all-over stretching program...

Indulge in a massage, acupuncture, acupressure, Reiki, saunas, hot tubs...

Dance, swing, waltz, do the boot scootin' boogie, bossa nova, hip hop till you drop, dance on a pole, whirl like a dervish...

Meditate, pray, chant, drum...

Board a boat, hoist a sail, row hard, kayak, shoot the rapids...

Go camping, watch birds and squirrels, listen, smell, stoke a crackling fire at midnight...

Cook up a big simmering pot of a comfort stew; grow flowers, vegetables, fruit, herbs, either outside or on a vacant window sill inside...

Travel, take day trips, week-long excursions, go for a month, or flip on the travel channel. Go where you have never gone before, experience different people, customs and cultures. Visit a barrio, drop into a castle...

Sun on your face, a breeze against your cheek, drift barefoot down a sandy beach; climb into some mountains; wander out into a desolate dry desert; hike through some woods, follow the bends and turns of a free-flowing river...

Make love at noon; laugh till your bladder leaks; play hard, sleep in, eat dessert, light candles. Listen to a symphony, the rain, leaves rustling in the wind, geese passing overhead and the sound of a train rumbling on through the middle of a dark night...

Read, write, make poems, paint, sing, sculpt, carve, whittle, join community theater, or while away an hour or a day just looking out a sparkling clean window...

Dream. Envision. Stay balanced, grounded and determined to go on making of this beautiful, but beleaguered planet, a sacred sanctuary.

CHAPTER TEN

Soulful Citizen Activists

The goal of life is to make your heartbeat match the beat of the universe, to match your nature with Nature.

Joseph Campbell

Somewhere along the way we've lost the plot. As part of this 13-billion-year-old pattern and sequence, we have lost what it means to be a human being. We have lost what it means to be a human being nestled within other living systems, part of the marvel and narrative and drama of an ever-expanding and complex universe. A universe in which all of it, and all of us, have wondrously unfolded from out of that long-ago single fiery event.

And now this hallowed world has been set on fire by those driven mad with greed and ignorance. Our shared world, with its shared lands, and seas, and air; lush with forests and flowers and sentient beings have nowhere to run, nowhere to hide from the senseless conquest, violence, and destruction.

We have been hustled, swindled, strong-armed, ripped off, hoodwinked, snookered, and sold down the river by those predators among us who believe they are more special than the rest, entitled to live as they so

113

please, to take whatever they want, to take what doesn't belong to them.

Sacred outrage, combined with controlled intentional purposeful nonviolent action, is a most appropriate response.

We have been taken prisoner, locked inside a cage, a consumer's world, where everything is commodified. We have been led to believe that everything fulfilling that a human being needs comes with a price tag. We have been deluded into believing that in this great big, beautiful, bountiful world there is not enough to go around, that there is a lack and a scarcity. It is that sort of wrong-headed thinking that has created great violence throughout the world.

To value and praise the hoarding of more money and more things over the cherishing of humans is living outside the universal laws of cooperation and connection. To value and praise the separation of ourselves from each other has interfered with how we have come to define ourselves as humans; it prevents us from assuming our proper place on earth.

We are in grave danger. They have come for our children and our grandchildren and are making of them a human sacrifice on the altars of greed and ignorance. The world is burning to the ground while too many are standing by dumb-struck and paralyzed by distractions, delusions, addictions, fear, despair, and hopelessness.

Sacred outrage and intentional action is a most appropriate response.

We have been stripped of our natural and rightful soul state of awe and wonder. We are in mortal danger and must now act quickly to bring the world into balance, into a place where living things can thrive and flourish in holy communion and cooperation with each other and all else; within all systems we intersect and upon whom we depend for survival.

As Andrew Harvey and Anne Baring write in *The Mystic Vision: Daily Encounters with the Divine:*

> The real war in the modern world is not between democracy and communism, or between capitalism and totalitarianism or between liberalism or fascism. It is the war for the mind and heart of humankind between two completely different versions of reality: the version that materialist science, most contemporary philosophy, and most modern art gives human beings, as driven, dying animals in a random universe (a version that many institutionalized religions unconsciously abet with their emphasis on human sinfulness and powerlessness) and that version of humankind's essential divine destiny that mystics in all ages have discovered and struggled to keep alive.[51]

I have had the great, good fortune to live abroad, and have flown back into the States countless times. It always brings tears to my eyes when I slog down the hallway into Customs, dazed, bone-tired from a long flight, and am greeted there by a smiling customs officer who says to me, "Welcome home."

Soulful Citizen Activists

Yes, America is a place of many different people living together but that is our greatest asset—our differences. In all its vast complexity, contradictions, and confusion, with all its faults, mistakes, missteps, missing the mark, and falling short, human freedom is still our highest calling.

The epitome of human freedom is to develop ourselves as individuals while caring for each other collectively.

Such high endeavors are never, ever neat, orderly, quiet, or without rigorous struggle and conflict.

I am compelled to use my time and energy to undo the misguided strangleholds and to instead, create a world that is a safe habitat not only for tender human beings, but for all those who call this earth Home.

This is my highest calling and that which I have pledged to devote my remaining days. As long as I have breath in my body and a light in my soul, I am claiming my very rightful place, in this fabric of time that I have been born, to uphold the values, principles, mission, and vision upon which this awesome universe first burst forth, with all its unfolding galaxies and stars and planets, with all its earthly-evolving life and with all its peoples and interconnecting systems.

I will keep tending this injured world, keep kissing the open wounds, honoring all those many, countless and marginalized people who came before, who suffered long and toiled hard to have us realize who we truly are: caring, compassionate, playful, sociable, party animals who love hanging out with each other, laughing and talking and learning from each other; helping each other; coming up with big ideas that will make all our lives better; who want to be free to smile and wave to our neighbors next door or on the next street or in another nation; knowing that we all share the same needs and desires; we all want to love and be loved, to take care of our children and our mates; we all just want to be our true and natural selves, cooperating and connecting as individuals and as members of a human family and as part of our larger Collective Soul.

Sacred Outrage, along with Soulful Citizen Action, is a most appropriate response to being thwarted and obstructed from living in our full and total innate state.

To take the world into one's arms and to act toward it in a soul-filled and soul-strengthening manner is a powerful act of wildish spirit.
One of the most calming and powerful actions you can do to intervene in a stormy world is stand up and show your soul. Struggling souls catch light from other souls who are fully lit and willing to show it.

Clarissa Pinkola Estés

WANTED: Seasoned Women

Spicy, saucy, marinated in years of lived experience and hard-won wisdom

Must possess a pioneering spirit and:
• be willing to get a few hairs singed while blazing new trails
• work well with other scorched and soulful activist pioneers
• chart new and unexplored territory
• dismantle the status quo

Responsibilities include:
• Answering your deep inner calling, the one that hounds you by day in your thoughts, and by night in your dreams, incessant, unrelenting, whispering, chanting, singing: "It's time. It's your time. To do your part.
• To make of this world a healthy, whole, hospitable, safe, sane, and sustainable home for our children and grandchildren."

Must have prior experience with:
• Feeling the impulse to fly
• Baying at the moon
• Running hard through thick underbrush
• Trembling with excitement
• Shaking to the core
• Burning brightly with fire and passion
• Yearning for deeper connection and meaning
• Fierce longings to expand and explore
• Deep-hearted feelings and a caring and compassion so strong that it breaks open your whole heart and your whole consciousness such that it can hold and cradle every man, woman, child, beast, bird, tree, ocean, river, rock and flower.

Must be able to:
• Walk long distances in the dark.
• Gather courage.
• Dare to act.
• Sustain it.
• Tolerate high levels of chaos, uncertainty, doubt, fear, criticism, joy, satisfaction, and happiness.
• Be present, and stay present, to the chaos and upheaval happening outside with others and inside with you; to the pain and suffering of others while managing your own inner emotions.

• Allow others to feel and express a full range of emotions. Rage. Despair. Anxiety. Depression. Fear. Grief over the loss of loved ones, a job, a home, financial solvency, retirement savings, credit ratings, lifestyle changes, climate changes, social and political uncertainty; global, economic, energy, and environmental catastrophes.
• Expect that the dark collective human Shadow will emerge in varying degrees of intensity and force. Resistance. Sabotage. Violence. Cruelty.

Must be committed to:
• Reaching for the highest, deepest, most complete expression of yourself.
• Recognize and manage the steps and stages of change and transformation, Life-Death-Life, this birthing of a better, new way of being in the world.
• Letting die what must die (outmoded ways of being in the world) and helping to birth what is emerging (a new way of being in relationship with each other and the earth).
• Building the kind of communities needed for survival and optimal existence for all.
• Staying the course, no matter the obstacles and challenges, towards bringing about the changes desired in the community.

Must be willing to:
• Get up off your fanny.
• Roll up your sleeves.
• Apply generous amounts of comfort, compassion, healing, and wisdom.

There is a tide in the affairs of men.
Which, taken at the flood, leads onto fortune;
Omitted, all the voyage of their life
Is bound in shallows and in miseries.

Soulful Citizen Activists

On such a full sea are we now afloat,
And we must take the current when it serves,
Or lose our ventures.

William Shakespeare[52]

The time is ripe! The need for action is now!

Gathering courage, daring to act, building the kind of communities that are a natural habitat in which humans can flourish.

The time is ripe and the need for passionate action is now, to change the narratives and the frames, to build the new human and consciously contribute to our evolution. As Mark Savio said in 1964:

> There is a time when the operation of the machine becomes so odious, makes you so sick at heart, that you can't take part; you can't even passively take part, and you've got to put your bodies upon the gears and upon the wheels, upon the levers, upon all the apparatus, and you've got to make it stop. And you've got to indicate to the people who run it, to the people who own it, that unless you're free, the machine will be prevented from working at all![53]

The path forward is understanding that the good life, our greatest joy and deepest need is based on setting free our innate compassionate natures and consciously contributing to each other's well-being.

Another world is not only possible, she is on her way. On a quiet day I can hear her breathing.

Arndhati Roy

Our culture; our worldview; the way we treat each other; the way we talk to each other; the way we judge and think about each other; the way we numb ourselves to the suffering of others; the denigration we receive from ourselves and others if we let ourselves feel any kind of feelings at all; are all a very sad and dangerous testament to our utter failure to learn the lessons the Universe has to teach us and the wisdom it has to offer us towards consciously participating in creation and evolution.

What does it mean to be human?

What is it we all share in common?

What would it be like to recover our time-honored practices of cooperation, loving relationships and community?

What would it be like to recover our innate ability to feel and practice compassion, and to acknowledge that compassion is at the central core of our humanness?

What would it be like to dare to feel deeply? To allow our full range of emotions, harnessing their energy and directing them as a force for good?

What would it be like if we allowed ourselves to feel, and speak of, the profound mystery of life and the ineffable wonder and awe of universal creation with all its interdependent and interconnecting systems, woven together, drawing together, coming together, in a never-ending pulse of attracting principles while expanding outward as one energetic expression of love?

What would our communities look like if we started from the basics of what it means to be a human nestled inside this sacred dance and then determine what we want as humans for ourselves and our children and our grandchildren?

What could our governments look like? Our businesses? Our Education and Health Care systems? Our faith communities? Legal systems? Media?

In *The Hidden Heart of the Cosmos,* Brian Swimme reveals the essential context, nature and purpose of what it means to be human:

> The universe is a single multiform event. There is no such thing as a disconnected thing. Each thing emerged from the primeval fireball, and nothing can remove the primordial link this establishes with every other thing in the universe, no matter how distant. You and everything you do and become are further articulations of the primal fireball...
>
> We were there in the distant, terrifying furnace of the primeval fireball. Not as mere witnesses, either, but as central to the event. Our bodies remember that event, exulting in the majesty of the night sky precisely because all suffered it together. The planet is a rare and holy relic of every event of twenty billion years of cosmic development.
>
> When we deepen our awareness of the simple truth that we are here through the creativity of the stars, we begin to feel fresh gratitude. When we reflect on the labor required for our life, reverence naturally wells up within us. Then, in the deepest regions of our hearts, we begin to

embrace our own creativity. What we bestow on the world allows others to live in joy. Such a stupendous mystery...!

Think of it. This supreme dynamic of love, of allurement and evocation, in action since the beginning of the universe, after billions of years becomes aware of itself. Life-enhancing and being evoking allurement knows itself, the magic of creating life and being now reflects upon its own mystery! What creatures, what living beings, what persons will follow us, entering life and the great mystery of love precisely because of our work![54]

There are things that need protecting. There are things that need defending so that they can survive.

NOTES

1. Pirkl, James J. 2009. "The Demographics of Aging." Transgenerational Design. transgenerational.org/aging/demographics.htm.
2. Meyer, Susan R. October 15, 2014. *Fifty Over Fifty: Wise and Wild Women Creating Wonderful Lives (And You Can Too!)* Booklocker.com, Inc.
3. Cicetti, Fred. August 2, 2013. "Does Happiness Increase As We Get Older?" www.livescience.com/38645-happiness-increase-get-older.html.
4. Estés, Clarissa Pinkola. 1992. *Women Who Run With the Wolves.* Ballantine Books New York, pp. 352-368.
5. Reich, Robert B. 2011. *Aftershock: The Next Economy & America's Future.* Vintage Books.
6. Ibid.
7. Hedges, Chris. "Let's get this Class War Started." Truthdig. October 20, 2013. www.truthdig.com/reportitem/lets_get_this_class_war_started_20131020/
8. Ibid.
9. Sharp, Gene. 2012. *From Dictatorship to Democracy.* The New Press, pp. 28-29.
10. Ibid., p. 31.
11. Lakoff, George. 2006. *Thinking Points: Communicating Our American Values and Vision.* Farrar, Straus and Girot.
12. Ibid.
13. Diamond, L. and McDonald, J. 1996. *Multi-Track Diplomacy: A Systems Approach to Peace.* Kumarin Press, pp. 5-6.
14. Ibid, p. 6.
15. Ibid.
16. Lakoff, George. 2008. *The Political Mind.* Viking, p. 267.

17. "Fifteen Core Issues the Country Must Face." 2011. Popular Resistance. Retrieved March 16, 2014. www.popularresistance.org/issues/.
18. Kretzmann, John P. and McKnight, John L. 1993. *Building Communities From the Inside Out: A Path Towards Finding and Mobilizing A Community's Assets.* Center for Urban Affairs and Policy Research; Neighborhood Innovations Network, p.110. Excerpt used with permission of the authors.
19. Ibid.
20. Ibid., pp. 19-24. Excerpts used with permission of the authors.
21. Mattessich, P., Monsey, B., and Roy, C. 1997. *Community Building: What Makes it Work: A Review of the Factors Influencing Successful Community Building.* St. Paul: Amherst H. Wilder Foundation.
22. Ibid., pp. 27-43.
23. Wheatley, Margaret J. 1994. *Leadership and the New Science.* Berrett-Koehler Publishers, Inc.
24. Ibid., pp. 132-135.
25. Mattessich, P., Monsey, B., and Roy, C. 1997. *Community Building,* op. cit., p. 25.
26. Ibid., p. 41.
27. Ibid., pp. 44-49.
28. Ibid.
29. Kretzmann, John P. and McKnight, John L. *Building Communities From the Inside Out,* op. cit., p. 34.
30. Kriesberg, Louis. 1997. "The Development of the Conflict Resolution Field," *Peacemaking in International Conflict: Methods and Techniques,* eds. I. William Zartman and J. Lewis Rasmussen, Washington DC: United States Institute of Peace Press, pp. 51-77; Miall, H., Ramsbotham, O., and Woodhouse, Tom. 2001. *Contemporary Conflict Resolution.* Polity Press, pp. 39-64.
31. Miall, H. et al., p. 51.
32. Moore, Christopher W. 2003. *The Mediation Process: Practical Strategies for Resolving Conflict.* Jossey Bass, pp. 20-22.
33. Barrett, Jerome T. and Barrett, Joseph. 2004. *A History of Alternative Dispute Resolution: The Story of a*

Notes

Political, Social and Cultural Movement. Jossey-Bass, pp. 1-6.

34.   Carpenter, Susan L., Kennedy, W.J.D., *Managing Public Disputes: A Practical Guide for Government, Business, and Citizens' Groups.* 2001. Jossey-Bass, pp. 3-17.

35.   Ibid, pp. 52-65.

36.   These 4 questions are from ibid., p. 80.

37.   Ibid., p. 102.

38.   Ibid.

39.   Ibid.

40.   Ibid.

41.   Ibid., pp. 67-154.

42.   Phelps, Joseph. 1999. *More Light, Less Heat: How Dialogue Can Change Christian Conflicts into Growth.* As cited in Schrock-Shenk, Carolyn, ed., *Mediation and Facilitation Training Manual: Foundations and Skills for Constructive Conflict Transformation. 4th edition.* 2000. Mennonite Conciliation Service, p. 207.

43.   "Global Education for Mission." Episcopal Church Center, 815 Second Ave., New York, NY 10017. As cited in Schrock-Shenk, Carolyn, ed., ibid., p. 206.

44.   "The Busy Citizen's Discussion Guides." Study Circles Resource Center. Everyday Democracy. www.everydaydemocracy.org. As cited in Schrock-Shenk, Carolyn, ed., ibid., p. 208. Excerpt used with permission of Everyday Democracy.

45.   www.urbandictionary.com/define.php?term=check+yourself.

46.   Smith, Sam. www.samsmitharchives.wordpress.com, January 21, 2015.

47.   Harvey, Andrew. 2009. *The Hope.* Hay House, Inc., pp. 92-99.

48.   Baring, Anne. 2013. *The Dream of the Cosmos*, Archive Publishing., p. 273.

49.   Estés, Clarissa Pinkola. 1992. *Women Who Run With the Wolves*, op. cit., pp. 63-64.

50.   Harvey, Andrew. 2009. *The Hope.* Hay House, Inc., pp. 173-178.

51. Baring, Anne and Harvey, Andrew. 1995. *The Mystic Vision: Daily Encounters with the Divine.* Harper San Francisco, p. 88.
52. William Shakespeare. *Julius Caesar*, Act 4, Scene 3, lines 218-224.
53. Savio, Mario. Talk at Sproul Hall, University of California, Berkeley, December 2, 1964.
54. Swimme, Brian. 2000. *The Hidden Heart of the Cosmos*. www.theconversation.org/archive/swimme.html.